SILVER BURDETT music

ELIZABETH CROOK
BENNETT REIMER
DAVID S. WALKER

SILVER BURDETT COMPANY

MORRISTOWN, NEW JERSEY · GLENVIEW, ILLINOIS
PALO ALTO · DALLAS · ATLANTA

SPECIAL CONTRIBUTORS

William M. Anderson (non-Western music), Aurora, Ohio
Kojo Fosu Baiden (music of Africa), Silver Springs, Maryland
Dulce B. Bohn (recorder), Wilmington, Delaware
Charles L. Boilès (music of Mexico), Bloomington, Indiana
Ian L. Bradley (Canadian music), Victoria, British Columbia, Canada
Gerald Burakoff (recorder), Levittown, New York
Henry Burnett (music of Japan), Flushing, Long Island, New York
Richard J. Colwell (testing and evaluation), Urbana, Illinois
Marilyn C. Davidson (music for Orff instruments), Bergenfield, New Jersey
Joan Davies (music of Canada and Japan), Charlottetown, P.E.I., Canada
Kay Hardesty (special education), Chautauqua, New York
James M. Harris (music in early childhood), San Francisco, California
Doris E. Hays (avant-garde music), New York City
Nazir A. Jairazbhoy (music of India), Windsor, Ontario, Canada
Maria Jordan (music of Greece), Hicksville, Long Island, New York
Robert A. Kauffman (music of Africa), Seattle, Washington
Edna Knock (music of Canada), Brandon, Manitoba, Canada
John Lidstone (visual arts), Brooklyn, New York
David McHugh (youth music), New York City
Alan P. Merriam (music of the North American Indians), Bloomington, Indiana
Lucille Mitchell (American folk songs), Alexandria, Virginia
Maria Luisa Muñoz (music of Puerto Rico), Houston, Texas
Lynn Freeman Olson (listening program), New York City
Mary E. Perrin (music in the inner city), Chicago, Illinois
Carmino Ravosa (children's song literature), Briarcliff Manor, New York
Joyce Bogusky-Reimer (avant-garde music), Wilmette, Illinois
Geraldine Slaughter (music of Africa), Washington, D.C.
Mark Slobin (music of the Near East), Middletown, Connecticut
Ruth Marie Stone (music of Africa), New York City
Leona B. Wilkins (music in the inner city), Evanston, Illinois

CONSULTANTS

Lynn Arizzi (levels 1 and 2), Reston, Virginia
Joy Browne (levels 5 and 6), Kansas City, Missouri
Nancy Crump, classroom teacher, Alexandria, Louisiana
Lyla Evans, classroom teacher, South Euclid, Ohio
Catherine Gallas, classroom teacher, Bridgeton, Missouri
Linda Haselton, classroom teacher, Westminster, California
Ruth A. Held, classroom teacher, Lancaster, Pennsylvania
Judy F. Jackson, classroom teacher, Franklin, Tennessee
Mary E. Justice, Auburn University, Auburn, Alabama
Jean Lembke (levels 3 and 4), Tonawanda, New York
Barbara Nelson, classroom teacher, Baytown, Texas
Terry Philips (youth music), New York City
Ruth Red, Director of Music Education, Houston, Texas
Mary Ann Shealy (levels 1 and 2), Florence, South Carolina
Beatrice Schattschneider (levels 1–6), Morristown, New Jersey
Paulette Schmalz, classroom teacher, Phoenix, Arizona
Sister Helen C. Schneider, Clarke College, Dubuque, Iowa
Merrill Staton (recordings), Alpine, New Jersey

ACKNOWLEDGMENTS

The authors and editors of SILVER BURDETT MUSIC acknowledge with gratitude the contributions of the following persons.

Marjorie Hahn, New York
Yoriko Kozumi, Japan
Ruth Merrill, Texas
Mary Ann Nelson, Texas
Bennie Mae Oliver, Texas
Joanne Ryan, New York
Helen Spiers, Virginia
Shirley Ventrone, Rhode Island
Avonelle Walker, New York

Credit and appreciation are due publishers and copyright owners for use of the following.

"Crossing" from LETTER FROM A DISTANT LAND by Philip Booth. Copyright 1953 by Philip Booth. Originally appeared in The New Yorker. Reprinted by permission of Viking Penguin Inc.

"Geranium" by Mary Ellen Solt from FLOWERS IN CONCRETE by Fine Arts Department, University of Indiana © 1966. Reprinted by permission of Mary Ellen Solt.

"Slowly" from THE WANDERING MOON by James Reeves. Used by permission of the publisher, William Heinemann Ltd.

"Tom and Joe" from AWAY AND AGO by David McCord. Copyright © 1968, 1971, 1972, 1973, 1974 by David McCord. Used by permission of Little, Brown and Co.

"Windy Winter Rain . . ." by Shisei-Jo, from JAPANESE HAIKU, p. 57. Copyright © 1955 Peter Pauper Press, Inc. Reprinted by permission.

CONTENTS

BEGINNING EXPERIENCES

Show rhythm by moving.

● *Run, Run, Run*

If you can move to the steady beat, you are ready to play the beat.

Steady beat:

Quarter notes:

Eighth notes:

Try playing a pattern of
quarter notes and eighth notes
to accompany *Run, Run, Run.*

Show rhythm by playing.

PAY ME MY MONEY DOWN

SLAVE SONG FROM THE GEORGIA SEA ISLANDS

COLLECTED AND ADAPTED BY LYDIA A. PARRISH

1. I thought I heard the cap - tain say,

"Pay me my mon - ey down, ___

To - mor - row is our sail - ing day, ___

Pay me my mon - ey down." _

REFRAIN

"Pay ___ me, ___ oh, pay ___ me, ___

Pay me my mon - ey down, ___

Pay me or go to jail, ___

Pay me my mon - ey down." _

Make up your own percussion accompaniment for this song. How many different rhythm patterns can you think of?

2. As soon as the boat was clear of the bar,
"Pay me my money down,"
He knocked me down with the end of a spar,
"Pay me my money down." *Refrain*

3. Well, I wish I was Mr. Steven's son,
"Pay me my money down,"
Sit on the bank and watch the work done,
"Pay me my money down." *Refrain*

Beginning Experiences 5

SCRATCH, SCRATCH

WORDS AND MUSIC BY HARRY BELAFONTE AND LORD BURGESS

1. Oh, we went out to a par - ty,

It was me and Ben and Mac,

And be - fore I knew what hap - pened,

I got an itch - in' on my back.

B REFRAIN

Scratch, scratch me back, Scratch, scratch me back.

It real - ly is a fact,___

The less I itch, the more I scratch.

2. Well, I was quite embarrassed,
   Till my two friends I did see,
   Well, they were madly itching,
   And they were screaming louder than me.
   Refrain

3. Now, this scratching was contagious,
   And it didn't take very long,
   Ev'rybody there was itching,
   As they joined me in this song.
   Refrain

Use sticks to play beats grouped in twos.

HAND GAME SONG   AMERICAN INDIAN SONG

Ha   a   a ho - e tha a, Ha   a   a ho - e tha a

Ha   a   a ho - e tha a, Ha   a   ho - e tha,

Ha   a   a ho - e tha a, Ha   a___ a ho - e tha a,

Ha   a___ a ho - e tha.

Try playing a different pattern.

Try doing a hand jive with this music.

⊙ Scruggs: *String Bender*   ⊙ Joplin: *Bethena*

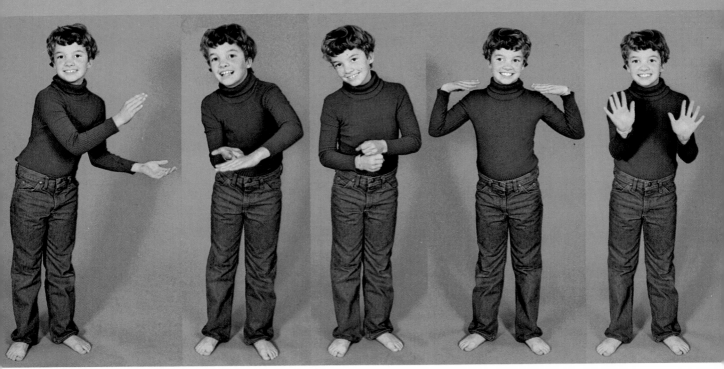

Can you hear the difference between meter in 2 and meter in 3?

HERE I GO   ROUND ⊙

FROM THE BOOK OF ROUNDS BY MARY CATHERINE TAYLOR AND CAROL DYK. COPYRIGHT © 1977 BY MARY CATHERINE TAYLOR. REPRODUCED BY PERMISSION OF E. P. DUTTON.

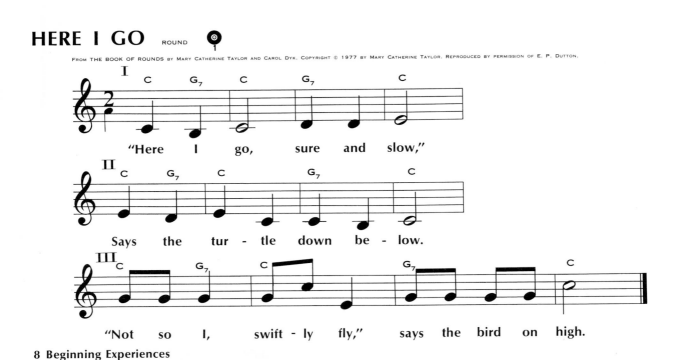

WHEN IS A DOOR?

WORDS AND MUSIC BY GEORGE F. ROOT

When is a door not a door? Give it up?

When is a door not a door? Let me see. Ah,

yes, when it is a - jar. _____

SANDY McNAB

ROUND

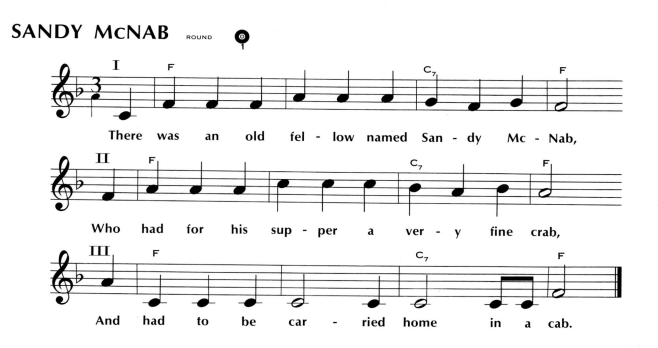

There was an old fel - low named San - dy Mc - Nab,

Who had for his sup - per a ver - y fine crab,

And had to be car - ried home in a cab.

Play low G and high G on the bells to accompany this song.

Will the meter be in 2, or in 3?

HEAR THE ROOSTER
Kum bahur FOLK SONG FROM ISRAEL ENGLISH WORDS BY ROSEMARY JACQUES

I
Hear the roost-er crow-ing, it's time to start the day,
Kum ba-hur a-tzel____ v'-tzei la-a-vo-da,

Hear the roost-er crow-ing, it's time to start the day.
Kum ba-hur a-tzel____ v'-tzei la-a-vo-da.

II
Wake, wake,____ get up with-out de-lay,
Kum, kum,____ v'-tzei la-a-vo-da,

Wake, wake,____ get up with-out de-lay.
Kum, kum,____ v'-tzei la-a-vo-da.

III
Ku-ku-ri-ku, ku-ku-ri-ku, let's be on our way,
Ku-ku-ri-ku, ku-ku-ri-ku, tar-n'-gol ka-ra,

Ku-ku-ri-ku, ku-ku-ri-ku, let's be on our way.
Ku-ku-ri-ku, ku-ku-ri-ku, tar-n'-gol ka-ra.

Find the repeated tones. Find the leaps.

Play 6 times.

high C

R. L.

C

G

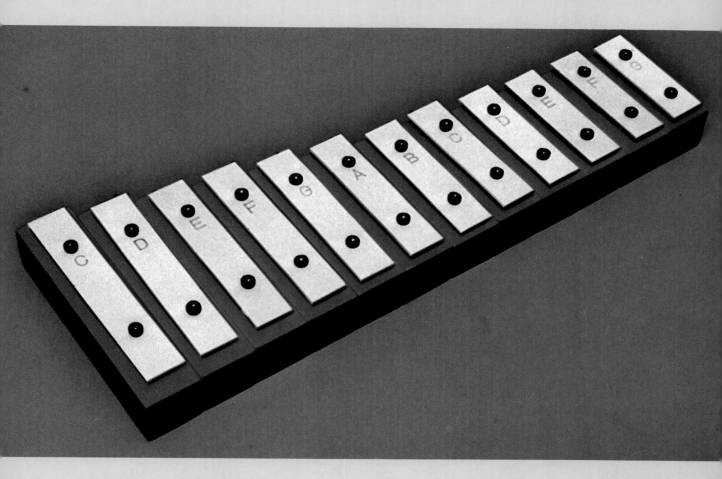

Find the tones that leap. Find the tones that step.

Play 2 times.

G E

D C

These melodies are endings of songs you know.

Can you name the songs?

Can you find things that remind you of steps, leaps, and repeats

in these pictures?

Here are three countermelodies to play with "Here I Go."

Which countermelody steps mostly downward?

Which one uses an octave leap?

Which one has mostly repeated tones?

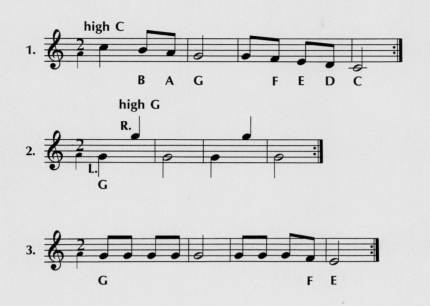

Which melody moves in an upward direction?

In a downward direction?

What does staff 3 show?

1.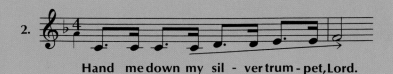

Hand me down my sil - ver trum-pet, Lord.

2.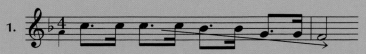

Hand me down my sil - ver trum - pet, Lord.

3.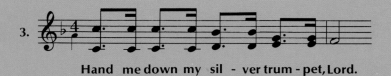

Hand me down my sil - ver trum - pet, Lord.

Find the places in "Hand Me Down" where upward

and downward directions are sung at the same time.

HAND ME DOWN   BLACK SPIRITUAL

SOLO   C₇   F

Oh,   hand   me down,   Hand   me down,

CHORUS   F   C₇

Hand   me down   my   sil - ver trum - pet, Ga - briel.

D.C. al Fine (Da Capo al Fine—Dah Kah′-poh ahl Fee′-nay) means

"repeat from the beginning and continue to the word *Fine*."

Show call-and-response form by singing.

SOURWOOD MOUNTAIN

AMERICAN FOLK SONG

SOLO
1. Chick - en crowin' on Sour - wood Moun - tain,
2. My true love's a blue - eyed dai - sy,

CHORUS
Hey de - ing dang did - dle al - ly day.

SOLO
So man - y pret - ty girls, I can't count 'em,
If I don't____ get____ her, I'll go cra - zy,

CHORUS
Hey de - ing dang did - dle al - ly day.

SOLO
My true love, she lives in Letch - er,
Big dog bark and lit - tle one bite you,

CHORUS
Hey de - ing dang did - dle al - ly day.

SOLO
She won't come and I won't fetch her,
Big girl court and lit - tle one slight you,

CHORUS
Hey de - ing dang did - dle al - ly day.

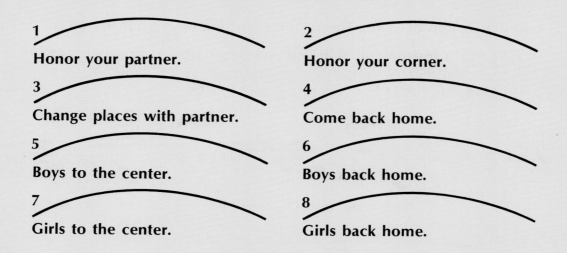

1 ‿‿‿
Honor your partner.

2 ‿‿‿
Honor your corner.

3 ‿‿‿
Change places with partner.

4 ‿‿‿
Come back home.

5 ‿‿‿
Boys to the center.

6 ‿‿‿
Boys back home.

7 ‿‿‿
Girls to the center.

8 ‿‿‿
Girls back home.

Couple

Couple 2

Couple 4

Head Couple

Choose a section of "Ging Gong Gooli" to sing or accompany on a percussion instrument. Will you choose section A, or section B?

GING GONG GOOLI
FOLK SONG FROM BRITISH GUIANA

Ging gong goo-li goo-li goo-li goo-li wat-cha,

Ging gong goo, ging gong goo.

Ging gong goo-li goo-li goo-li goo-li wat-cha,

Ging gong goo, ging gong goo.

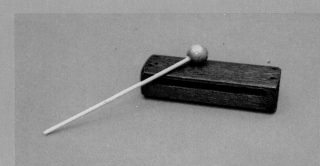

Wood Block

Ⓐ

Drum

Hai - la,_____ hai - la shai - la,_____

Shai - la hai - la shai - la ho - la - ho!

Hai - la,_____ hai - la shai - la,_____

Shai - la hai - la shai - la ho!_____

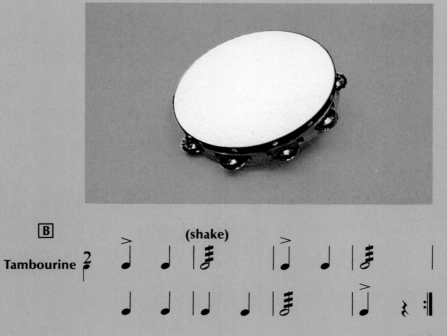

B

Tambourine

(shake)

LOOK

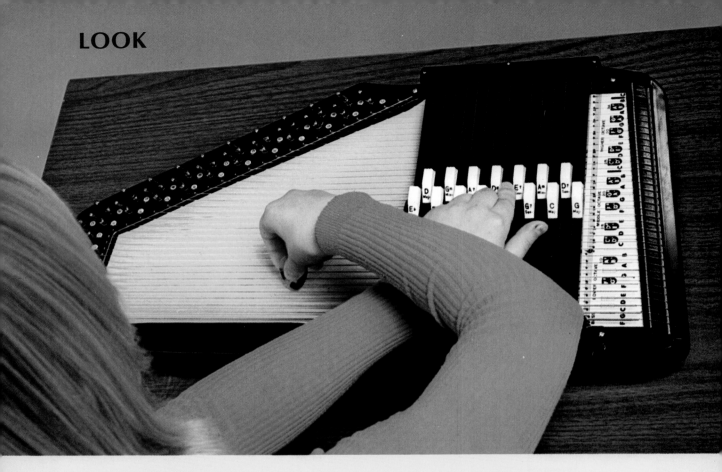

LISTEN

The Wise Man Built His House

PLAY

- Place your left index finger on the button marked F.
- Place your left middle finger on the button marked C_7.
- Look at the chord pattern below. It shows when to press each button.
- As you press the buttons, use your right hand to strum the strings.
- Make each strum last for two beats.
- Follow the chord pattern to play as others sing "The Wise Man Built His House." You will be playing half notes.

$$F \qquad C_7 \qquad C_7 \qquad F$$

THE WISE MAN BUILT HIS HOUSE

ORIGIN UNKNOWN

3. Oh, the silly man built his house upon the sand, (*3 times*)
   And the rains came tumbling down.

4. Oh, the rains came down and the floods came up, (*3 times*)
   And the house on the sand went swisssssssssssh.

Play this chord pattern on the Autoharp to accompany "Sambalele."

SAMBALELE
FOLK SONG FROM BRAZIL WORDS BY RUTH AND THOMAS MARTIN

(A) VERSE

1. Hear how the mu - sic is play - ing,
2. Dance while the drum - beat is pound - ing,

Dance to its light - heart - ed mea - sures,
Mel - low gui - tars soft - ly strum - ming,

Clap - ping and stamp - ing and sway - ing,
And cas - ta - nets clear - ly sound - ing,

Join in the car - ni - val plea - sures.
Join in the whis - tling and hum - ming.

Add a percussion accompaniment for section A.

Castanets
or Maraca
(struck against
palm of hand)

Sam - ba, sam - ba, sam - ba - la - le - le,

While we are danc - ing and sing - ing so gai - ly,

Sam - ba, sam - ba, sam - ba - la - le - le,

While we are danc - ing and sing - ing so gai - ly.

Add a percussion accompaniment for section B.

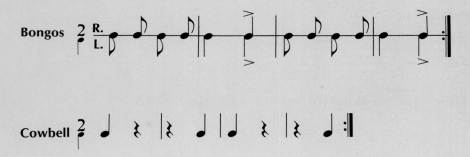

Bongos

Cowbell

Here is a countermelody to sing or play throughout section A or B,

or throughout the entire song.

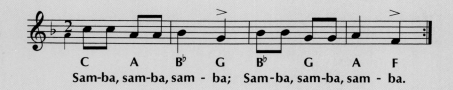

C   A   B♭   G   B♭   G   A   F

Sam-ba, sam-ba, sam - ba; Sam-ba, sam-ba, sam - ba.

Sing this part throughout section A.

Voice

Sit down, Broth-er.   Sit down, Broth-er.

OH, WON'T YOU SIT DOWN? BLACK SPIRITUAL

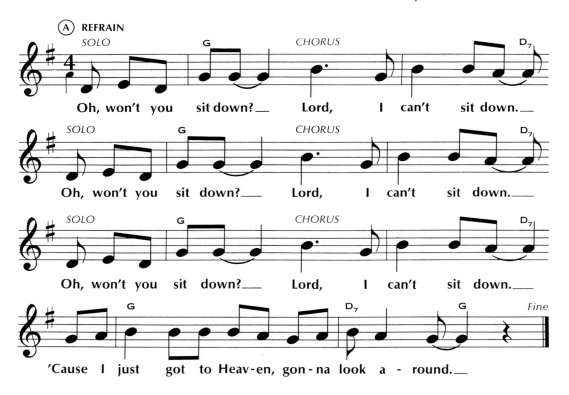

Ⓐ REFRAIN

SOLO   G   CHORUS   D₇

Oh, won't you   sit down? __   Lord,   I   can't   sit down. __

SOLO   G   CHORUS   D₇

Oh, won't you   sit down? __   Lord,   I   can't   sit down. __

SOLO   G   CHORUS   D₇

Oh, won't you   sit down? __   Lord,   I   can't   sit down. __

G   D₇   G   Fine

'Cause I just   got to Heav-en, gon-na look a - round. __

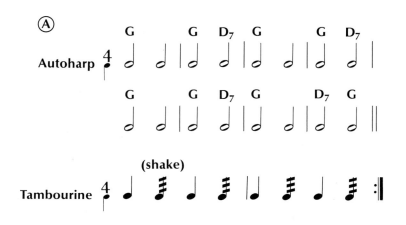

Ⓐ

G   G D₇ G   G D₇

Autoharp

G   G D₇ G   D₇ G

(shake)

Tambourine

Sing this part throughout section B.

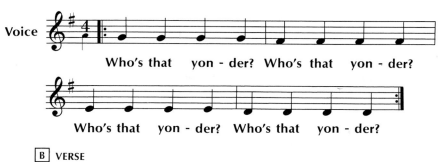

Voice

Who's that yon - der? Who's that yon - der?

Who's that yon - der? Who's that yon - der?

B VERSE

SOLO
G

1. Who's that yon - der dressed in red?___

CHORUS
G   D₇   G

Must be the chil - dren that___ Mo - ses led.___

SOLO
G

Who's that yon - der dressed in white?___

CHORUS
G   D₇   *D.C. al Fine* G

Must be the chil - dren of the Is - rael - ite._____

2. Who's that yonder dressed in blue?

   Must be the children that are comin' through.

   Who's that yonder dressed in black?

   Must be the hypocrites a-turnin' back. *Refrain*

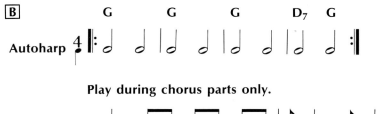

B   G   G   G   D₇   G

Autoharp

Play during chorus parts only.

Wood Block

LOOK

LISTEN

**Listen to the tone color
of a group of recorders,
called a consort.**

⊚
1
  Widmann, Erasmus: *Margaretha*

PLAY

G

How to Play G

1. Using your left hand, cover the holes shown in the diagram.

   Press just hard enough so the holes make a light mark on your fingers.

2. Cover the tip of the mouthpiece with your lips. Blow gently

   as you whisper "daah."

Play G throughout a song you know.

Hear the Rooster, Version 2

Now try playing G, A, and B.

Your recorder notes look like this.

Your fingers should cover these holes.

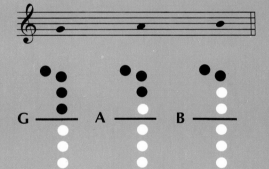

Play a recorder part for "Ging Gong Gooli." It uses G, A, B.

Practice playing some melodies that use B, A, G on the recorder.

HOT CROSS BUNS TRADITIONAL

AT PIERROT'S DOOR FOLK MELODY FROM FRANCE

MERRILY WE ROLL ALONG TRADITIONAL

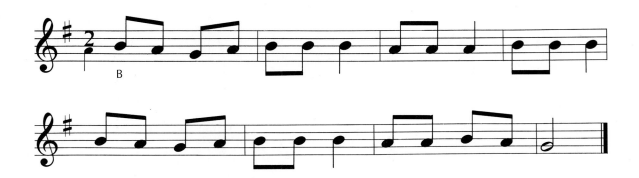

Playing an instrument in a group is one of the most pleasant

kinds of music making. Try adding the recorder parts below

to the percussion and Autoharp parts

on pages 24 and 25.

Play this recorder countermelody during section A of

"Oh, Won't You Sit Down?" It uses B, A, G.

Here is a countermelody to play during section B.

It also uses B, A, G.

Sing the rhyming words when they come in this song.

MICHAEL FINNEGAN   CHILDREN'S GAME SONG

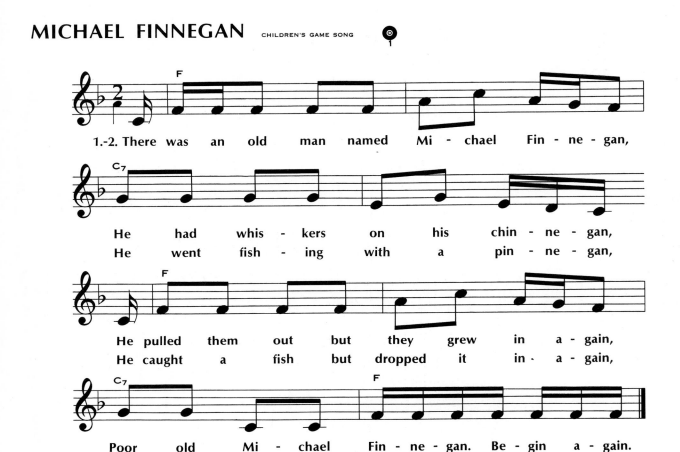

1.-2. There was an old man named Mi - chael Fin - ne - gan,

He had whis - kers on his chin - ne - gan,
He went fish - ing with a pin - ne - gan,

He pulled them out but they grew in a - gain,
He caught a fish but dropped it in - a - gain,

Poor old Mi - chael Fin - ne - gan. Be - gin a - gain.

3. There was an old man named Michael Finnegan,

   Climbed a tree and barked his shinnegan,

   He lost about a yard of skinnegan,

   Poor old Michael Finnegan. Begin again.

4. There was an old man named Michael Finnegan,

   He grew fat and then grew thinnegan,

   Then he died and that's the endegan,

   Poor old Michael Finnegan. Begin again.

When you sing a melody alone, there is no harmony.

This drawing shows a melody alone.

When you play chords to accompany a melody, there is harmony.

This drawing shows a melody with chords.

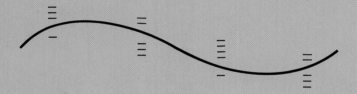

Play chords to accompany "Michael Finnegan."

You know that when chords accompany a melody there is
harmony.

Two melodies that fit together also make harmony.

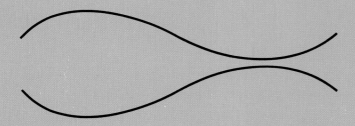

Here is a countermelody that can be sung with "Michael Finnegan."

Countermelody

F   E   D   C
Mi - chael Fin - ne - gan,   Mi - chael   Fin - ne - gan,

G
Mi - chael Fin - ne - gan,   Mi - chael   Fin - ne - gan,

Mi - chael Fin - ne - gan,   Mi - chael   Fin - ne - gan,

high C

B♭   A
Poor   old   Mi - chael   Fin - ne - gan.

WHAT DO YOU HEAR? 1: TEXTURE

Listen to these pieces.

For each one, choose the symbol that best describes the texture.

If you hear melody alone, choose  .

If you hear melody with chords, choose  .

If you hear two or more melodies together, choose .

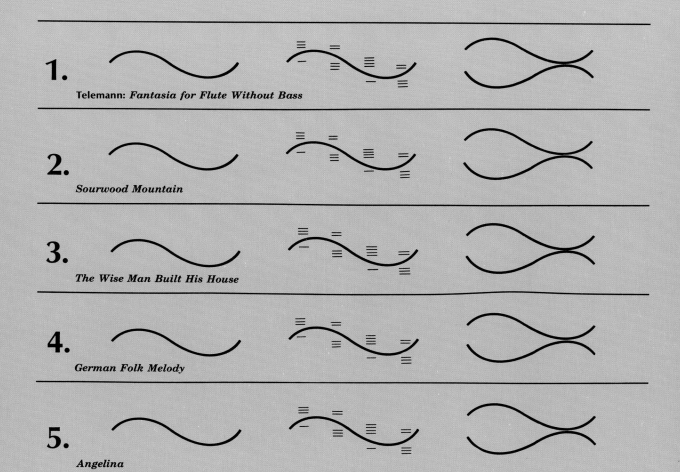

1.
   Telemann: *Fantasia for Flute Without Bass*

2.
   Sourwood Mountain

3.
   The Wise Man Built His House

4.
   German Folk Melody

5.
   Angelina

LISTENING TO MUSIC

What part of you lets you hear the sounds of this music?

CALL CHART 1: LISTENING TO MUSIC

As your ears hear sounds, your mind tells you what the sounds are doing. How many of these things is your mind aware of? The numbers will help you listen carefully.

Bizet: *L'Arlésienne Suite No. 1*, Overture

---

1. *THEME:* **Strings play together.**

---

2. *VARIATION 1:* **Soft; woodwinds play.**

---

3. *VARIATION 2:* **Gets louder and softer.**

---

4. *VARIATION 3:* **Slower; theme smooth; accompaniment has short tones.**

---

5. *VARIATION 4:* **Like a march; drums play.**

---

6. *CODA (ending section):* **Loud, soft, ends softly.**

The more <u>sounds</u> your <u>ears</u> <u>hear</u>, and the more sounds your <u>mind</u> is <u>aware</u> of, the more your <u>feelings</u> can <u>respond</u>.

An orchestra is making the sounds of this music.

Paintings give a feeling of movement.

Which painting seems to be more active?

Which painting seems to be more still?

Why?

Music also gives a feeling of movement. Which piece seems
to be more active? Which piece seems to be more still?

Gershwin: *An American in Paris*   Ives: *The Pond*

Both painting and music seem to have movement.

Some paintings and some music have active movement—others are still.

Each art creates a sense of movement differently, so each art gives
its own special feeling.

TEMPO

Choose your own tempo for "Flea!" Will it be fast? Moderate? Slow?

Will the tempo get faster? Will it get slower?

Clapping Pattern:

FLEA! ECHO CHANT

© 1978 PACHYDERM MUSIC, CAPAC

LEADER   GROUP   LEADER   GROUP

Flea!   Flea!   Flea - fly!   Flea - fly!

LEADER   GROUP

Flea - fly mos-qui - to!   Flea - fly mos-qui - to!

LEADER, then GROUP

Oh,   no,   no,   no_____ more   mos - qui - toes,

LEADER, then GROUP

Itch - y,   itch - y, scratch - y, scratch - y,

Oo,   I got   one down   my back - y,

LEADER, then GROUP   ALL

Beat   that   big   bad   bug   with   the   bug   spray.   Tshsh_

How does the tempo change in "Dayenu"?

Does it get faster, or slower?

DAYENU

HEBREW PASSOVER SONG   ENGLISH WORDS BY ELIZABETH S. BACHMAN

Ⓐ VERSE

1. He has led us out of E - gypt, led His peo - ple out of E - gypt,

He has led us out of E - gypt, *da - ye - nu.*

Ⓑ REFRAIN
gradually getting faster (accelerando)

Da - da - ye - nu,_____ da - da - ye - nu,_____

Da - da - ye - nu, da - ye - nu da - ye - nu da - ye - nu,

Da - da - ye - nu,_____ da - da - ye - nu,_____

Da - da - ye - nu, da - ye - nu da - ye - nu.

2. He has given us the Sabbath, given us the holy Sabbath,
   He has given us the Sabbath, *dayenu. Refrain*

3. He has given us the Torah, given us the blessed Torah,
   He has given us the Torah, *dayenu. Refrain*

How does the tempo change in "Lazy Coconut Tree"?

Does it get faster, or slower?

LAZY COCONUT TREE

MUSIC BY DOUGLAS COOMBES   WORDS BY JOHN EMLYN EDWARDS

FROM TA-RA-RA-BOOM-DE-AY. PUBLISHED BY A & C BLACK LTD. REPRINTED BY PERMISSION OF DAVID HIGHAM ASSOCIATES LIMITED.

1. Some folk like to go fish - ing____ far a - cross the bay,
2. I could be a rich mer - chant____ in some fine ba - zaar,

I would rath - er be dream - ing____ on the beach all day.
But I'd rath - er be hap - py____ nod - ding to a star.

(optional harmony part)

Like the la - zy co - co-co - co-nut, co - co-co - co-nut tree,

gradually getting slower (rallentando)

Like the la - zy co - co-co - co-nut, co - co-co - co-nut tree.

This song has three sections—A, B, C. How is the tempo different in each one?

DRY BONES   BLACK SPIRITUAL

A
E - ze - kiel cried, "Them   dry bones!" E - ze - kiel cried, "Them   dry bones!"

E - ze - kiel cried, "Them   dry bones!" Now hear   the word   of   the Lord.

B
gradually getting faster

The   foot   bone   con - nect - ed   to   the   leg   bone,

The   leg   bone   con - nect - ed   to   the   knee   bone,

The   knee   bone   con - nect - ed   to   the   hip   bone,

The   hip   bone   con - nect - ed   to   the   back   bone,

The   back   bone   con - nect - ed   to   the   shoul - der bone,

The   shoul - der bone   con - nect - ed   to   the   neck   bone,

The   neck   bone   con - nect - ed   to   the   jaw   bone,

The jaw bone con-nect-ed to the head bone,

Now hear the word of the Lord.

fast

Them bones, them bones gon-na walk a-round, Them bones, them bones gon-na

walk a - round, Them bones, them bones gon - na walk a - round,

getting slower last time

Now hear the word of the Lord.

CALL CHART 2: TEMPO

Here are selections from a set of pieces.

Listen for the tempo in each piece.

As each number is called, look at the chart.

It will help you hear what the beat is doing.

Satie: *Sports et Divertissements*

1. *SLOW* ("CHANT")

2. *FAST* ("FIREWORKS")

3. *MODERATE* ("SEE-SAW")

4. *FAST* ("THE HUNT")

5. *MODERATE* ("FISHING")

Some music makes you want to move.

Try some "fancy stepping" with this song.

I'M GONNA WALK

WORDS AND MUSIC BY DAVID EDDLEMAN

Piano acc., p. 277

I'm gon-na put, put, put on my walk-in' shoes, I'm gon-na but-, but-, but-ton up my coat, I'm gon-na walk right a-cross the land, there's lots o' things to see, And if you wan-ta you can walk with me.___ Oh, yes, I'm gon-na walk to the East,___ Walk to the West,___ Walk to the North and South;___ The

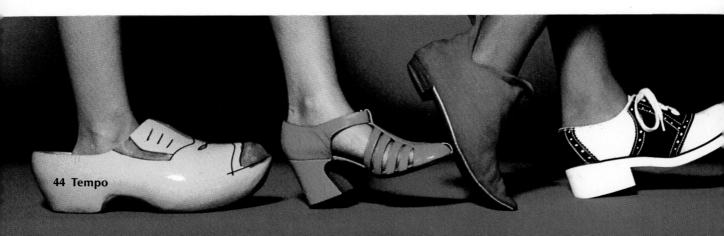

one thing that I love ____ the best ____ Is walk - in' all a - bout. ____ Well, ____ I'm gon - na put, put, put on my walk - in' shoes, I'm gon - na but-, but-, but - ton up my coat, I'm gon - na walk right a - cross the land, there's lots o' things to see, And if you wan - ta you can walk with me, ____ Walk with me, ____ Walk with me, ____ Walk with ____ me.

Find the place in the music where the beat stops and holds.

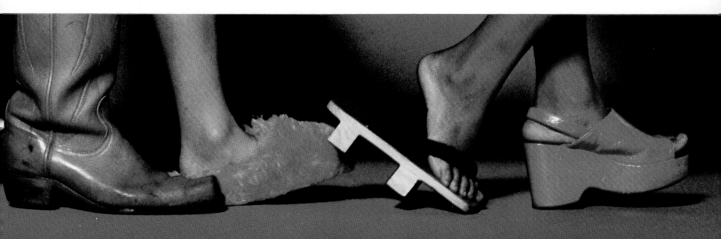

SOUND PIECE 1: Chance Music WYNN CHECK

Select a tempo by chance.

fast   slow   moderate

Select a time span by chance.

5"   10"   15"   20"

Example:

10"	15"	5"	20"
fast	*moderate*	*slow*	*moderate*

Play a section from a cassette tape in the tempo and time span you have chosen.

To perform a complete piece with others, select the order, by chance, in which you will play.

WHAT DO YOU HEAR? 2: TEMPO 🔊

Each time a number is called, decide which of the two answers is correct.

Choose the answer that best describes what is happening in the music.

Dvořák: *Slavonic Dances*, Op. 46, No. 7

1.	FAST	SLOW
2.	GETTING FASTER	GETTING SLOWER
3.	FAST	SLOW
4.	GETTING FASTER	GETTING SLOWER
5.	FAST	SLOW

Stravinsky: *Fireworks*

1.	FAST	SLOW
2.	FASTER	SLOWER
3.	GETTING FASTER	GETTING SLOWER

WHAT DO YOU HEAR? 3: TEMPO 🔊

Choose the word that best describes the tempo. Is it fast, or slow?

Do you hear the beat stop and hold? If you do, choose the fermata sign ⌒.

If you do not, choose no ⌒.

1.	FAST ⌒	SLOW NO ⌒	Haydn: *Symphony No. 104*, Movement 1
2.	FAST ⌒	SLOW NO ⌒	Beethoven: *Violin Concerto*, Movement 3
3.	FAST ⌒	SLOW NO ⌒	*Weary of the Railway*

THINGS PEOPLE
DO WITH MUSIC

Musicians at work

Hale Smith

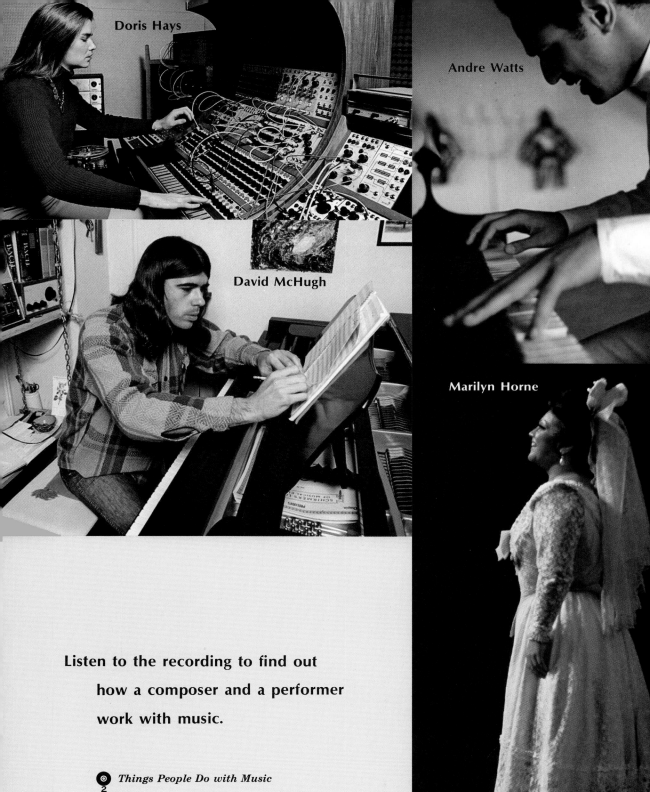

Doris Hays

Andre Watts

David McHugh

Marilyn Horne

Listen to the recording to find out
how a composer and a performer
work with music.

🔘 *Things People Do with Music*
2

DIRECTION

There is direction in things we *see*.
There is direction in music we *hear*.

Can you see direction in notation?

1.

G
Sit down, Broth - er,

2.

C
Hand me down my sil - ver trum-pet, Lord.

3.

D
Pay me or go to jail,___ Pay me my mon-ey down."

When you catch on to the form of this song, join in
with the recording.

I KNOW AN OLD LADY
MUSIC BY ALAN MILLS   WORDS BY ROSE BONNE

1. I know an old la - dy who swal-lowed a fly; I don't know why she

swal-lowed a fly! I guess she'll die.___ 2. I

know an old la - dy who swal-lowed a spi - der that wrig-gled and wrig-gled and

tick-led in - side her; She swal-lowed the spi - der to catch the fly, But

I don't know why she swal-lowed the fly. I guess she'll die! ___ I

bird! Now, how ab - surd, to
cat! Now, fan - cy that, to
know an old la - dy who swal-lowed a dog! My, what a hog, to
goat! Just opened her throat and
cow! I don't know how she

No repeat first time

swal - low   a   bird!   3.   She swal-lowed the bird   to   catch   the   spi - der
swal - low   a   cat!   4.   She swal-lowed the cat   to   catch   the   bird,— *(To 3)*
swal - low   a   dog!   5.   She swal-lowed the dog   to   catch   the   cat, — *(To 4)*
swal-lowed a   goat!   6.   She swal-lowed the goat   to   catch   the   dog,— *(To 5)*
swal-lowed a   cow!   7.   She swal-lowed the cow   to   catch   the   goat,— *(To 6)*

that wrig-gled and wrig-gled and tick-led   in - side her, She swal-lowed the spi-der to

catch   the   fly,   But   I   don't know why   she swal-lowed the   fly;

Verses 3–6.   *Verse 7.*

I   guess   she'll   die!_____   I   die!_____   8. I

(spoken)

Know an old   la - dy who swal-lowed a horse; She's dead,   of course!

Here are two ways to play and sing part of the song.

Which staff shows tones that move upward?   Downward?

1. C   D   E   F
I   guess she'll die._____

2. C   B   B♭   A
I   guess she'll die._____

FISHERMAN'S SONG

CALYPSO MELODY   WORDS BY WILLIAM ATTAWAY

WORDS FROM CALYPSO SONG BOOK BY WILLIAM ATTAWAY. COPYRIGHT © 1957 BY REBUS PUBLISHING CO. COPYRIGHT ASSIGNED © 1957 TO CALYPSO MUSIC, INC. USED BY PERMISSION.

3. Fisherman's lady got a dimple knee,

    Weigh up, Susianna,

    She boil her porgy with rice and peas,

    Round the Bay of Montserray. *Refrain*

CLOUDS

MUSIC BY HOAGY CARMICHAEL   WORDS BY CHRISTINA ROSSETTI

White sheep, white sheep, high on a wind-y hill,

When _____ the wind stops, you all stand still;

But_ when_____ the wind blows, you walk a-way slow.

Oh, white sheep, white sheep, where do you go?

Countermelody 1

high C

B   A   G   F   E   D

Countermelody 2

A   G   F   E   D   C

Follow the direction of the melody as you sing.

Which phrases move mostly downward?

Mostly upward?

LOUIS MOVED AWAY

MUSIC BY JIM HUNTER   WORDS BY TOM PAISLEY

Lou - is____ moved____ a - way to - day;____

Lou - is____ was____ my____ friend.____

Him and____ me____ would al - ways____ play,____

He al - ways had some bread to____ spend.____   (bell part)

His dad - dy makes good_____ pay;_____

That's what they all_____ say._____

And now I'll nev - er have a_____ friend,_____

'Cause Lou - is moved a - way._____

'Cause Lou - is moved a - way._____

'Cause Lou - is moved a - way._____

Play the last three phrases on bells or piano. They start on low A.

In which direction will you play?

Find phrases that move mostly upward or mostly downward in these songs.

    "Hand Me Down," page 14

    "Sourwood Mountain," page 16

    "The Wise Man Built His House," page 21

WHEN THE SAINTS GO MARCHING IN

BLACK SPIRITUAL

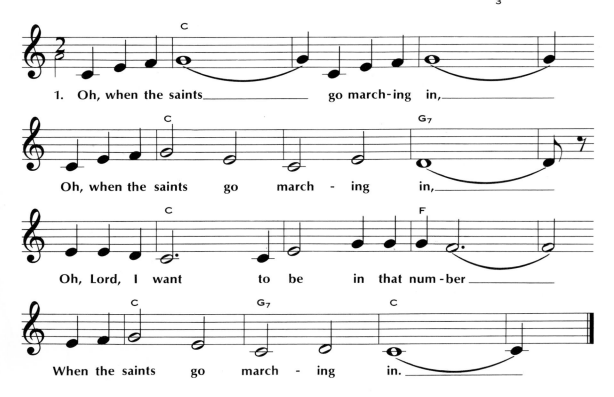

1. Oh, when the saints _____ go march-ing in, _____

Oh, when the saints go march - ing in, _____

Oh, Lord, I want to be in that num -ber _____

When the saints go march - ing in. _____

2. Oh, when the stars refuse to shine, . . .

3. Oh, when I hear that trumpet sound, . . .

Play the recorder as others sing.

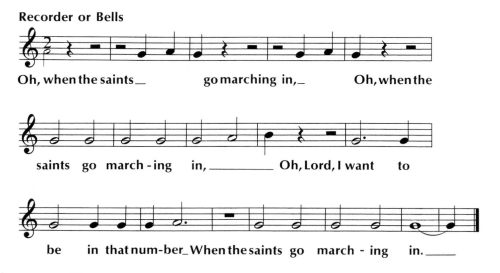

Recorder or Bells

Oh, when the saints ___ go marching in, ___ Oh, when the

saints go march - ing in, _____ Oh, Lord, I want to

be in that num-ber ___ When the saints go march - ing in. ____

Drum

HARVEST TIME

WORDS AND MUSIC BY GRACE C. NASH

FROM MUSIC WITH CHILDREN, JUNIOR CHOIR with ORFF INSTRUMENTS by MURRAY McNAIR and GRACE C. NASH, by special permission of GRACE C. NASH.

Har - vest is the sea - son to be - hold.

Har - vest with its col - ors brown and gold.

Crops are in and sum - mer work is done.

Air is crisp and snow is soon to come.

Har - vest is the sea - son to be - hold.

Ostinato 1

Ostinato 2

E

D

Sing this part throughout the song.

Ostinato

Boom, boom, boom, boom-dee-ah - da

I LOVE THE MOUNTAINS   TRADITIONAL

I love the moun - tains, I love the roll - ing hills,

I love the flow - ers, I love the daf - fo - dils,

I love the fire - side When all the lights are low,

Boom - dee - ah - da, boom - dee - ah - da, Boom - dee - ah - da, boom - dee - ah - da,

Boom - dee - ah - da, boom - dee - ah - da, Boom - dee - ah - da, boom - dee - ah - da.

CODA

Boom did - dle - dee - dum - dum, Boom, boom.

SOUND PIECE 2: Contours at the Keyboard

DAVID S. WALKER

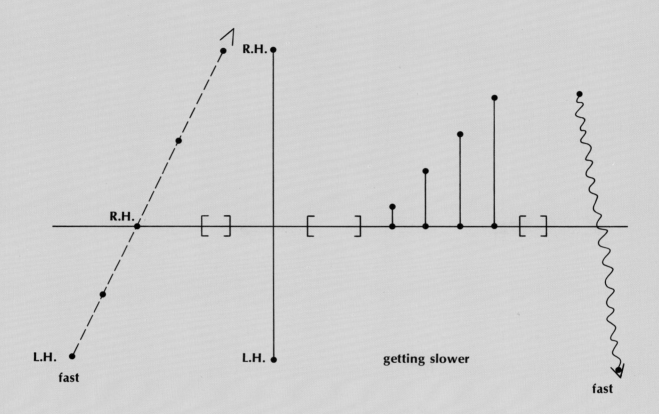

Here is the contour of the first phrase of a patriotic song.

Can you guess what it is?

For the answer, turn the page.

Follow the contour as you sing this melody.

THE STAR-SPANGLED BANNER

MUSIC BY JOHN STAFFORD SMITH   WORDS BY FRANCIS SCOTT KEY

Oh,___ say! can you see, by the dawn's ear - ly light,

What so proud - ly we hailed at the twi - light's last gleam - ing,

Whose broad stripes and bright stars, through the per - il - ous fight,

O'er the ram - parts we watched were so gal - lant - ly stream - ing?

And the rock - ets' red glare, the bombs burst - ing in air,

Gave proof through the night that our flag was still there.

Oh, say, does that___ Star - Span - gled Ban - ner___ yet___ wave___

O'er the land_____ of the free and the home of the brave.

62 Direction

CALL CHART 3: DIRECTION ⊚₃

Trace the upward and downward arrows with your finger each time you hear section A. The arrows show how the violin swoops upward and downward.

Paganini: *Caprice No. 5 in A Minor,* Op. 1

---

1. *SECTION A (UPWARD THEN DOWNWARD)*

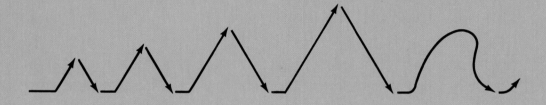

---

2. *SECTION B (BOTH UPWARD AND DOWNWARD)*

---

3. *SECTION A REPEATS.*

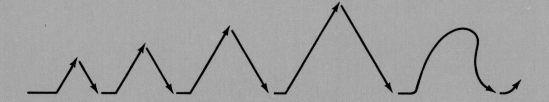

How does the melody move when you sing the words *Go, tell it on the mountain?*

GO, TELL IT ON THE MOUNTAIN

BLACK SPIRITUAL

A VERSE

Freely

1. When I was a seek - er, I sought both night and day.
2. He made me a watch - man Up - on the cit - y wall.
3. In the time of Da - vid, Some said he was a king.

I asked the Lord to help me, And He shows me the way.____
And if I serve Him tru - ly, I am the least of all.____
And if a child is true born, The Lord will hear him sing.____

B REFRAIN *(in rhythm)*

Go, tell it on the moun-tain, O - ver ___ the hills and ev - 'ry - where.

COUNTERMELODY

Go, tell it on the moun-tain,

Go, tell it on the moun-tain, Our heav'n - ly Lord ____ is born.

Go, tell it on the moun-tain, our Lord is born.

Listen to these pieces. Choose the answer that describes

the direction in which the melody is mostly moving.

---

1. UPWARD   DOWNWARD   BOTH UPWARD
AND DOWNWARD

Beethoven: *Symphony No. 1*, Movement 1

---

2. UPWARD   DOWNWARD   BOTH UPWARD
AND DOWNWARD

The Star-Spangled Banner

---

3. UPWARD   DOWNWARD   BOTH UPWARD
AND DOWNWARD

Poulenc: *Mouvement Perpétuel No. 1*

---

4. UPWARD   DOWNWARD   BOTH UPWARD
AND DOWNWARD

Cowell: *Advertisement*

---

5. UPWARD   DOWNWARD   BOTH UPWARD
AND DOWNWARD

Mussorgsky: *Pictures at an Exhibition:* "The Little
Hut on Chicken's Legs"

---

6. UPWARD   DOWNWARD   BOTH UPWARD
AND DOWNWARD

Paganini: *Caprice No. 5 in A Minor*

Were you able to hear the difference in direction?

If you can *hear* the difference, you can *feel* the difference.

STYLE

Do the poems on these pages look
as if they are in the same style,
or in different styles?

CROSSING

STOP LOOK LISTEN
as gate stripes swing down,
count the cars hauling distance
upgrade through town:
warning whistle, bellclang,
engine eating steam,
engineer waving,
a fast-freight dream:
B&M boxcar,
boxcar again,
Frisco gondola,
EIGHT-NINE-TEN,
Erie and Wabash,
Seaboard, U.P.,
Pennsy tankcar,
TWENTY-TWO, THREE,
Phoebe Snow, B&O,
THIRTY-FOUR, FIVE,
Santa Fe cattle
shipped alive,
red cars, yellow cars,
orange cars, black,
Youngstown steel
down to Mobile
on Rock Island track,

FIFTY-NINE, SIXTY,
hoppers of coke,
Anaconda copper,
hotbox smoke,
EIGHTY-EIGHT,
red-ball freight,
Rio Grande,
Nickel Plate,
Hiawatha,
Lackawanna,
rolling fast
and loose,
NINETY-SEVEN,
coal car,
boxcar,
CABOOSE!

Philip Booth

SLOWLY

Slowly the tide creeps up the sand,
Slowly the shadows cross the land.
Slowly the cart-horse pulls his mile,
Slowly the old man mounts the stile.

Slowly the hands move round the clock,
Slowly the dew dries on the dock.
Slow is the snail—but slowest of all
The green moss spreads on the old brick wall.

James Reeves

Listen to hear what makes
the poems different in style.

 Crossing   *Slowly*

Poems can be in different styles. Music can be in different styles, too.
Listen to these pieces to discover the differences between them—
the things that tell you they are in different styles.

Mozart: *Cassation in B^b*, Menuetto No. 1

Schoenberg: *Five Pieces for Orchestra*, No. 1

How many things can you hear that make the style of one piece
different from that of the other?

There are different ways of planning poems and music to create
different styles. Each style has its own special way of feeling.

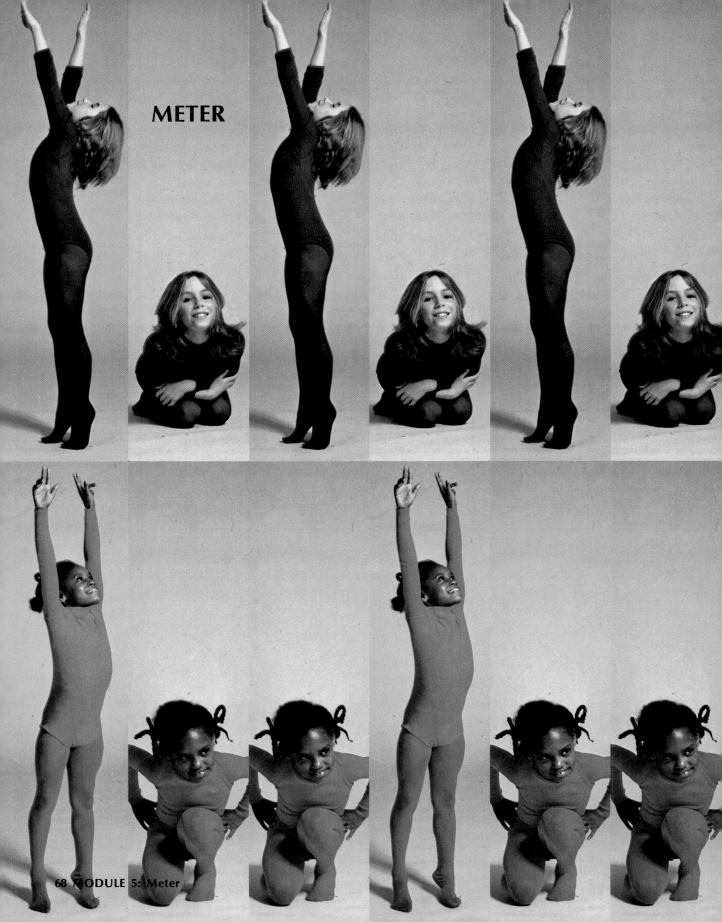

METER

Meter 69

Are the beats in this singing game grouped in sets of two,

or in sets of three?

SASA ABEREWA   SINGING GAME FROM AFRICA

FROM AFRICAN SONGS AND GAMES FOR CHILDREN COMPILED AND TRANSCRIBED BY KOJO FOSU BAIDEN AND GERALDINE SLAUGHTER. © 1970, KOJO FOSU BAIDEN AND GERALDINE SLAUGHTER.

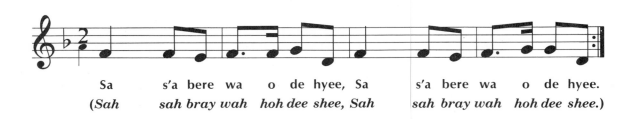

Sa   s'a bere wa   o de hyee, Sa   s'a bere wa   o de hyee.
(Sah   sah bray wah hoh dee shee, Sah   sah bray wah   hoh dee shee.)

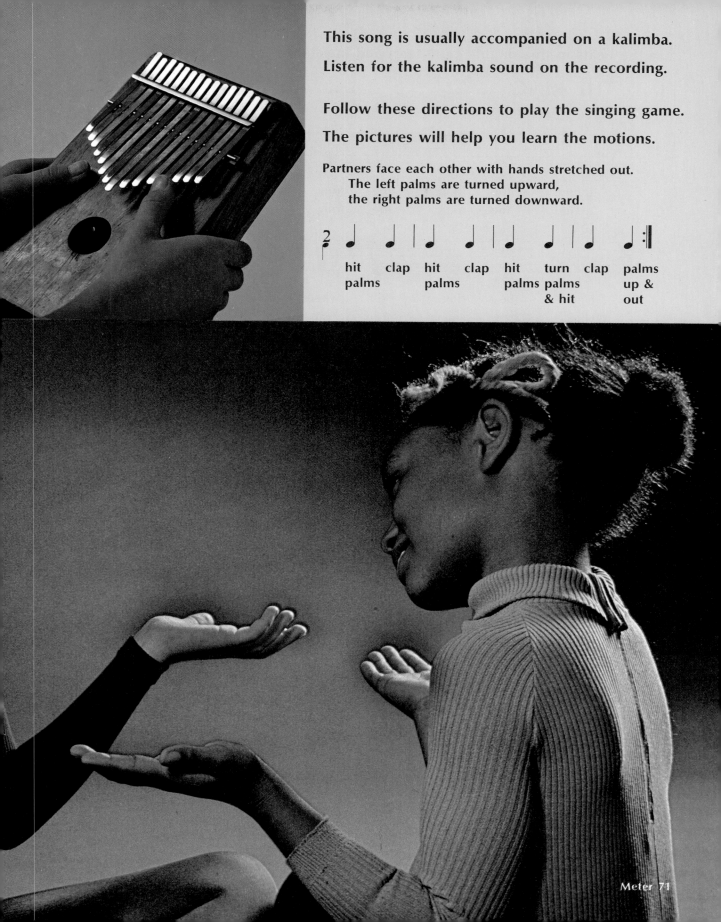

This song is usually accompanied on a kalimba.

Listen for the kalimba sound on the recording.

Follow these directions to play the singing game.

The pictures will help you learn the motions.

Partners face each other with hands stretched out.
 The left palms are turned upward,
  the right palms are turned downward.

| hit palms | clap | hit palms | clap | hit palms | turn palms & hit | clap | palms up & out |

Are the beats in this singing game grouped in sets of two, or in sets of three?

FIND THE RING

FOLK SONG FROM GREECE   ENGLISH WORDS BY MARIA JORDAN

(optional harmony part)

1. Find the ring, the ring that keeps mov - ing,
2. Find the ring, the ring that keeps mov - ing,

Find the ring, oh, where did it go?
Find the ring of sil - ver or gold.

The se - cret ring's in some - bod - y's hand, Some -
Pass it to me, I'll pass it to you, We

bod - y you know, come guess if you can!
must - n't get caught, what - ev - er we do!

Don't say a word if you are the one, Don't

give it a - way and spoil all the fun!

Play one of these patterns on a tambourine as others sing.

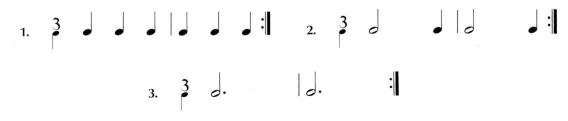

Play a game with "Find the Ring." Form a circle and follow these motions to pass the ring from one to the other.

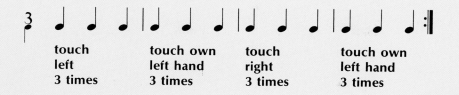

| touch
left
3 times | touch own
left hand
3 times | touch
right
3 times | touch own
left hand
3 times |

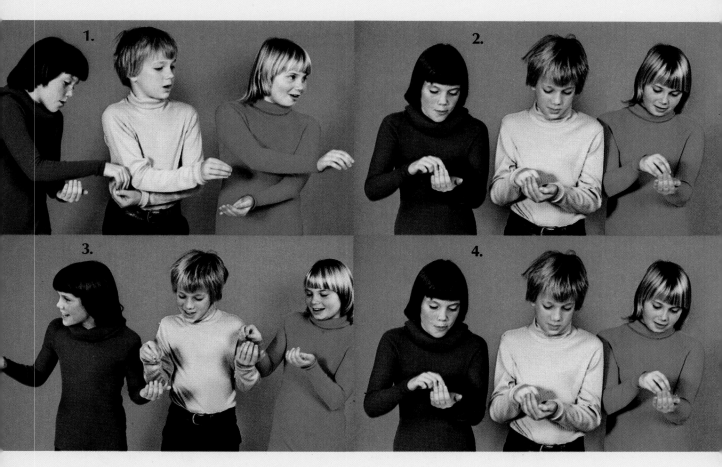

Play this part on recorder or bells as others sing and play the game.

Recorder or Bells

SOUND PIECE 3: DID SID?

DORIS HAYS © 1979 DORIS HAYS

SOUND PIECE 4: BUSY LIZZY

DORIS HAYS © 1979 DORIS HAYS

Liz was so bus - y, she was diz - zy,

Bus - y Liz - zy, Bus - y Liz - zy,   Bus - y Liz - zy, Bus - y Liz - zy, Bus - y Liz - zy,

in a tiz - zy,   Liz   was   bus - y,   Liz was in a   bus - y, fiz - zy tiz - zy,

Bus - y Liz - zy,   Bus - y Liz - zy, Bus - y   Liz - zy, Bus - y   Liz - zy, Bus - y Liz - zy,

Bus - y Liz - zy!

Bus - y Liz - zy.

Feel meter in 3 by playing this tambourine part with the recording.

Tambourine

(shake)

MANANA

FOLK SONG FROM SPAIN   COLLECTED AND ADAPTED BY BEATRICE LANDECK   ENGLISH WORDS BY ROSEMARY JACQUES

Ma - ña - na, por____ la ma - ña - na pa -
Ma - ña - na, por____ la ma - ña - na I____

sas - te, Jua - na, por____ mi ta - ller, la ran le.
stood there, Look - ing down____ at the street, la ran le.

Te ju - ro que____ ten - go ga - na de____
When Juana passed by____ with her twin - kling eye,____

ver - te, Jua - na, la____ pun - ta el pie.____
I just saw the toes____ of her feet.____

Now play another pattern in three meter.

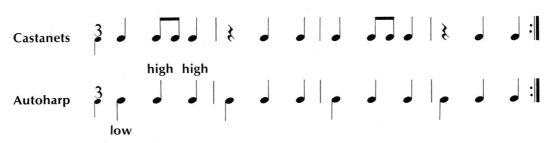

Castanets

high high

Autoharp

Feel meter in 4 by strumming this low-high pattern on the strings of the Autoharp.

high high high

low

A GREAT BIG SEA
FOLK SONG FROM NEWFOUNDLAND

FROM OLD TIME SONGS AND POETRY OF NEWFOUNDLAND. REPRINTED BY PERMISSION OF GERALD S. DOYLE LTD.

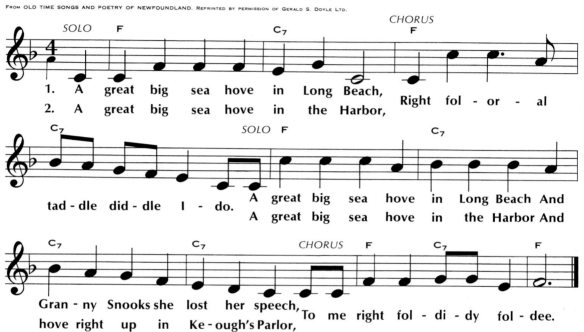

SOLO F   C₇   CHORUS F

1. A great big sea hove in Long Beach,
   Right fol - or - al
2. A great big sea hove in the Harbor,

C₇   SOLO F   C₇

tad - dle did - dle I - do. A great big sea hove in Long Beach And
A great big sea hove in the Harbor And

C₇   C₇   CHORUS F   C₇   F

Gran - ny Snooks she lost her speech, To me right fol - di - dy fol - dee.
hove right up in Ke - ough's Parlor,

3. "Oh, mother dear, I wants a sack,"   With beads and buttons down the back,"
   Right fol-or-al taddle diddle I-do.   To me right fol-didy fol-dee.
   "Oh, mother dear, I wants a sack

Play these four-meter patterns on the low- and high-C bells.

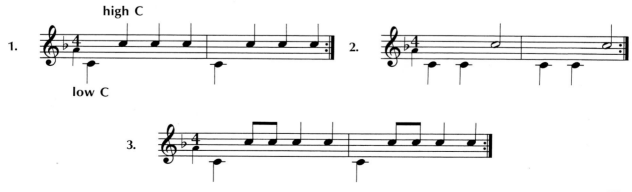

high C

1.

low C

2.

3.

Play beats in sets of four on a wood block.

Make the first beat of each set stronger than the others.

Now practice making the fourth beat silent.

Wood Block Pattern

Play the wood block pattern along with the recording.

Balkan Hills Schottische

You have played the rhythm of a dance called the *schottische*.

To dance a schottische, walk forward on the first three beats of
the measure and hop on the fourth beat. Begin with either
foot. Make your movements match the meter of the music.

Schottische step

step step step hop step step step hop

Vary the schottische step this way.

step hop step hop step hop step hop

Play beats in sets of three on a tambourine. Make the first beat
of each set stronger than the others.

Now shake the tambourine on beat 3 of each set.

Tambourine

hit   hit shake hit   hit shake hit   hit shake
elbow

Play the tambourine pattern along with the recording.

The Unhappy Cuckoo

You have played the rhythm of a dance called the *mazurka*.

To dance a mazurka, walk forward on the first two beats of the
measure and hop on the third beat. Begin with either foot.
Make your movements match the meter of the music.

Mazurka
step   step step hop step step hop step step hop

Try the mazurka step, stepping sideways to the left or to the right.

Tap this polka rhythm as you listen to the recording.

step   slide   step   hop   step   slide   step   hop

Emilia Polka

Dance the polka step throughout section B of this song.

IN BAHIA TOWN

FOLK SONG FROM BRAZIL   ENGLISH WORDS BY VERNE MUÑOZ

MELODY FROM FOLK SONGS AND DANCES OF THE AMERICAS, PUBLISHED BY THE GENERAL SECRETARIAT OF THE ORGANIZATION OF AMERICAN STATES.

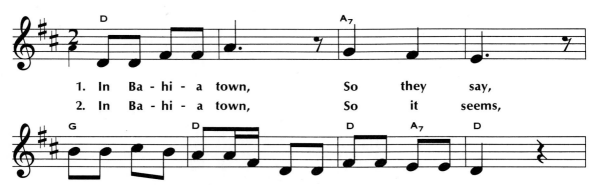

1. In Ba - hi - a town,   So   they   say,
2. In Ba - hi - a town,   So   it   seems,

They sell co - co - nuts for a pen - ny In the mar - ket place.
You can buy a sew - ing ma - chine That stitch - es like a dream.

In Ba - hi - a town,   So   they   say,
In Ba - hi - a town,   So   it   seems,

They sell fish that's bet - ter than an - y You will ev - er taste.
You can buy a lamp made of glass In shades of blue and green.

La la la la la la la la la, La la la la la la la,

La la la la la la la la la, La la la la la la.

WHAT DO YOU HEAR? 5: METER ⊚4

Can you hear meter in this music?

Listen to the recording to discover whether the meter

is in 2 or in 3.

---

1. *METER IN 2*   *METER IN 3*   Stravinsky: *Suite No. 2 for Small Orchestra,* "Valse"

---

2. *METER IN 2*   *METER IN 3*   Bizet: *Carmen Suite,* "March of the Street Urchins"

---

3. *METER IN 2*   *METER IN 3*   Gershwin: *An American in Paris*

---

4. *METER IN 2*   *METER IN 3*   Dvořák: *Slavonic Dances,* Op. 46, No. 6

---

5. *METER IN 2*   *METER IN 3*   Scruggs: *String Bender*

---

6. *METER IN 2*   *METER IN 3*   Saint-Saëns: *Carnival of the Animals,*
"The Elephant"

MODERN STYLES

These are two modern paintings.

What makes them different in style?

How are they alike?

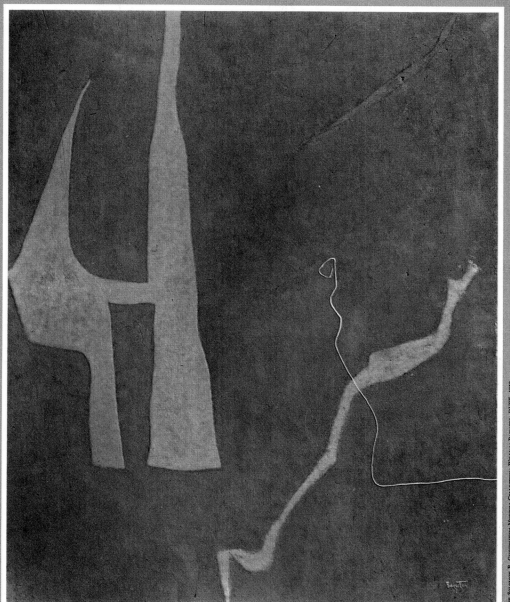

Modern Styles 83

These are two modern pieces of music. As you listen,
follow the words that show what makes these
pieces different in style. How are these pieces
alike?

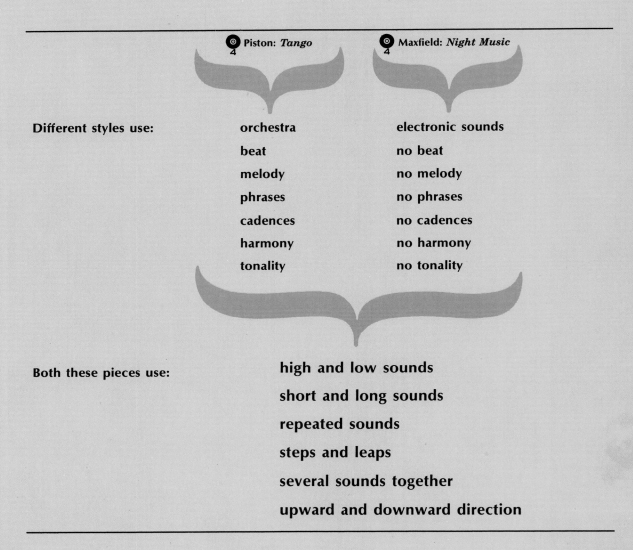

◎ Piston: *Tango*
4

◎ Maxfield: *Night Music*
4

Different styles use:

orchestra	electronic sounds
beat	no beat
melody	no melody
phrases	no phrases
cadences	no cadences
harmony	no harmony
tonality	no tonality

Both these pieces use:

high and low sounds

short and long sounds

repeated sounds

steps and leaps

several sounds together

upward and downward direction

◎ Copland: *Celebration*
4

◎ Babbitt: *Ensembles for Synthesizer*
4

Modern painting and modern music have many
styles. Some things are different in different
styles, but some things are the same no matter
what the style.

GERANIUM

Mary Ellen Solt

DYNAMICS

What do these pictures show about volume?

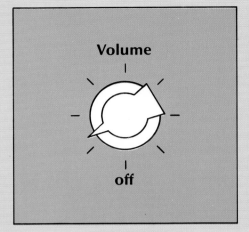 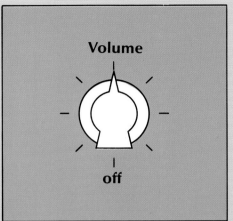 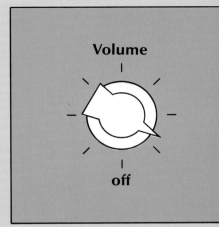

 Tom and Joe

TOM AND JOE

Tom loves to be heard;
Joe not at all.
Boom!
Can you hear Joe's small
voice? No? It seems to have died!
Boom!
You can hear *that*, though?
Yes? Well, *I told you so!*
I imply—I've implied;
You infer—you've inferred
that I'm *not* on Tom's side,
nor on Joe's. My one word
is: *Don't* be a Tom
who explodes like a bomb.
And oh, yes: on the other
hand, *Don't* be a Joe!

David McCord

 The Hi-Dee-Ho Man

Will you sing this music soft (p), moderately loud (mf), or loud (f)?

UP THE STREET THE BAND IS MARCHING DOWN

WORDS AND MUSIC BY LUIGI ZANINELLI

I *f*

Up the street the band is march-ing down,

II

Hear the fi - fers shrill, See the drum-mer's skill,

III

Tramp, tramp, tramp, round the town, round the town;

IV

If the trum-pets make an er - ror, See their fac - es pale with ter - ror.

AFRICAN RHYTHM COMPLEX

Say the numbers in each line below. Clap each time
you say a large-size number.

1 2 3 4 5 6 7 8 9 10 11 12

1 2 3 4 5 6 7 8 9 10 11 12

1 2 3 4 5 6 7 8 9 10 11 12

1 2 3 4 5 6 7 8 9 10 11 12

Now use percussion instruments to play the rhythms you clapped.
Follow the notation on p. 89.

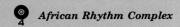 *African Rhythm Complex*

Here is the notation for the rhythms you clapped.

Bell 1

high
low

1 3 5 6 8 10 12

Bell 2

low

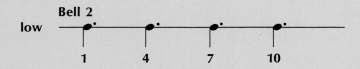

1 4 7 10

Rattle

hand
knee

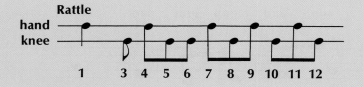

1 3 4 5 6 7 8 9 10 11 12

High Drum

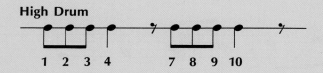

1 2 3 4 7 8 9 10

gankogui   **axatse**   **kagan**

Play these patterns on a tambourine when you sing "Dundai."

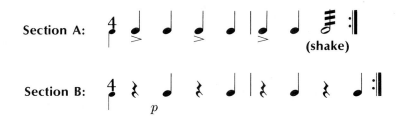

Section A:

(shake)

Section B:

p

DUNDAI

HEBREW FOLK SONG   ENGLISH WORDS BY HAROLD AKS

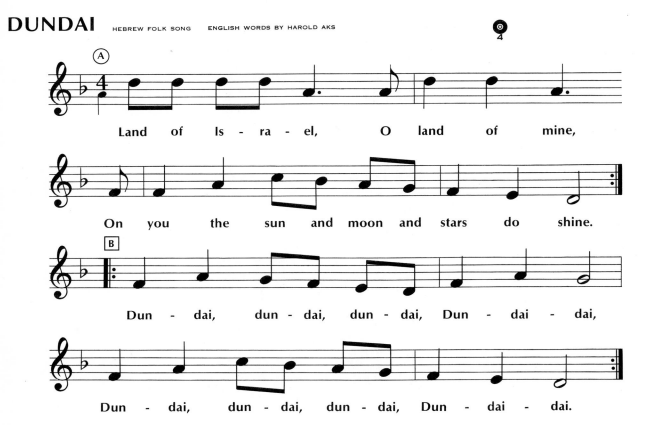

Land of Is - ra - el, O land of mine,

On you the sun and moon and stars do shine.

Dun - dai, dun - dai, dun - dai, Dun - dai - dai,

Dun - dai, dun - dai, dun - dai, Dun - dai - dai.

Sing this ostinato throughout section A.

Ostinato 1

Dun - dai, dun - dai, dun - dai, dun - dai

Play this ostinato during section B.

Recorder
or
Bells

Ostinato 2

How are dynamics used in this music? Listen to the recording. As each number is called, look at the chart. It will help you hear the changes in dynamics.

CALL CHART 4: DYNAMICS ◎₄

Ward: *America, the Beautiful*

1.	*MF*	*(MODERATELY LOUD)*
2.	*P*	*(SOFT)*
3.	◁	*(GETTING LOUDER)*
4.	*P*	*(SOFT)*
5.	◁	*(GETTING LOUDER)*
6.	*P*	*(SOFT)*
7.	*MF*	*(MODERATELY LOUD)*
8.	◁	*(GETTING LOUDER)*

Play these tambourine parts during "Ging Gong Gooli." Be certain to follow the dynamic markings.

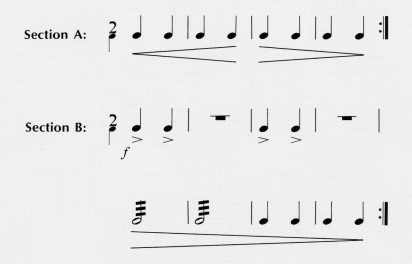

REMEMBER ME

BLACK SPIRITUAL

VERSE

mf

1. When chill - y winds blow from the North,___ I've got to go;
2. I've got a home in glo - ry land,___ out - shines the sun;

p

When chill - y winds blow from the North,___ I've got to go;
I've got a home in glo - ry land___ out - shines the sun;

mf

When chill - y winds blow from the North,___ I've got to go;
I've got a home in glo - ry land___ out - shines the sun;

f

A - way up be - yond ___ the moon.

REFRAIN

(optional harmony part)

Do, Lord, O do, Lord, O do re - mem - ber me;

Do, Lord, O do, Lord, O do re - mem - ber me;

Do, Lord, O do, Lord, O do re - mem - ber me;

f

A - way up be - yond ___ the moon.

WHAT DO YOU HEAR? 6: DYNAMICS

Listen to these pieces. Each time a number is called,

decide which of the three answers is correct.

Choose the answer that best describes what is happening in the music.

1. PIANO	FORTE	<>	**1.** PIANO	FORTE	<>
2. PIANO	FORTE	<>	**2.** PIANO	FORTE	<>
3. PIANO	FORTE	<>	**3.** PIANO	FORTE	<>

Mendelssohn: *Symphony No. 5*, Mvt. 2   Bizet: *Scènes Bohémiennes*, No. 3

WHAT DO YOU HEAR? 7: DYNAMICS

Listen to these pieces. Choose the answers that best describe the dynamics.

Is the music all soft? All loud? Soft and loud?

Do you hear accents? If you do, choose the word *accents*.

If you do not, choose the words *no accents*.

1. ALL P	ALL F	P AND F	ACCENTS	NO ACCENTS
				Stockhausen: *Klavierstück*
2. ALL P	ALL F	P AND F	ACCENTS	NO ACCENTS
				Ives: *The Pond*
3. ALL P	ALL F	P AND F	ACCENTS	NO ACCENTS
				Olantunji: *Jin-Go-Lo-Ba*
4. ALL P	ALL F	P AND F	ACCENTS	NO ACCENTS
				Alkan: *Les Diablotins*

FORM

Shapes and letters can show form in music.

Which shapes and letters show the form of songs you know?

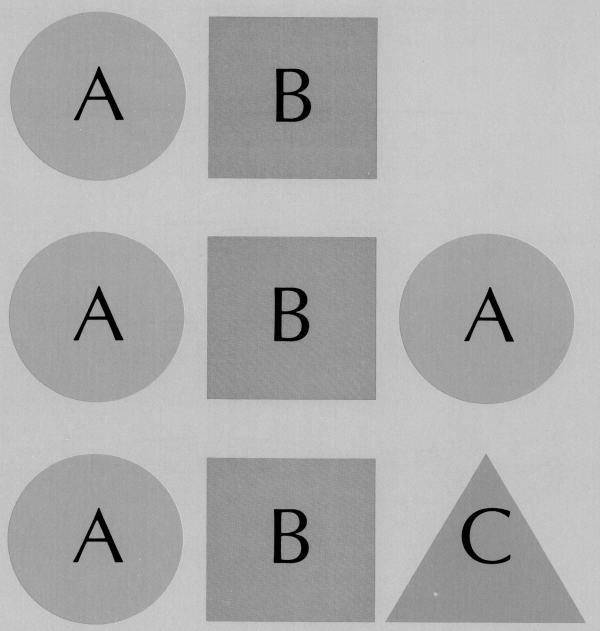

This song has two sections, A and B. How are they different?

SANDS GET INTO YOUR SHOES

WORDS AND MUSIC BY ARTHUR CARTER

USED BY PERMISSION.

1. You have - n't lived____ in the sum - mer - time____
2. The sun comes beat - ing down on your head,____

Un - til you've gone____ to the beach,____
The dust gets in - to your eyes,____

And tast - ed ice - cream: the lem - on lime,____
Your feet they hurt,____ but the thing you dread's____

Ba - na - na, wal - nut and peach.
The mos - qui - toes____ and the flies.

(optional harmony part)

And sands, and sands, and sands get in - to your o - pen shoes,

And sands, and sands, and sands get in - to your shoes.

3. You leave your things by the waterside,
And then somehow you forget
To move them back from the rising tide—
Your towels and blanket get wet.
And sands . . .

Play these percussion parts during section A.

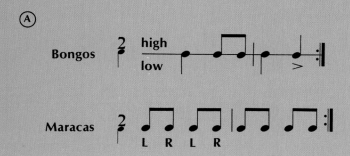

Here are parts to play during section B.

This dance music has two sections, A and B. Use movement to show the contrast between the sections.

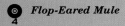 *Flop-Eared Mule*
4

This song has repetition and contrast. Find the place in the score that tells you section A repeats.

RUN, RUN, RUN

WORDS AND MUSIC BY CHRIS DEDRICK

© 1972 ALMITRA MUSIC COMPANY, INC.

Play this part on recorder or bells when it comes in the song.

It uses G and A.

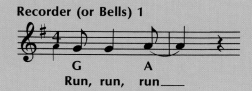

Recorder (or Bells) 1

G   A

Run, run, run____

To play more of section A, you will need two new tones—high C and D.

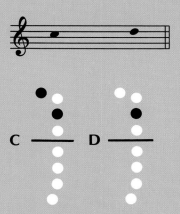

C ——— D ———

Now try playing this part during section A.

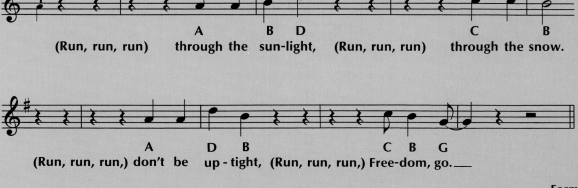

Recorder (or Bells) 2

A   B D   C   B

(Run, run, run)   through the sun-light,   (Run, run, run)   through the snow.

A   D B   C B G

(Run, run, run,) don't be   up-tight, (Run, run, run,) Free-dom, go.____

Listen to discover repetition and contrast in the sections of

this song. Is the form AB, or ABA?

DON'T COUNT YOUR CHICKENS

WORDS AND MUSIC BY CARMINO RAVOSA

© 1971 Carmino Ravosa

Violin

(Introduction)

Don't count your chick-ens be-fore they hatch, Be-fore they hatch,

be-fore they hatch. Don't count your chick-ens be-fore they hatch,

Be-fore they hatch, (clap   clap) they   hatch!

Don't you plan a-bout to-mor-row,'cause to-mor-row does-n't come un-til to -

mor - row;   Have a lot-ta fun to-day be-cause to -

mor-row may just bring a lot-ta sor - row. Don't you sor - row.

Don't count your chick-ens be - fore they hatch, Be - fore they hatch,

be - fore they hatch. Don't count your chick-ens be - fore they hatch,

Be - fore they hatch, (*clap clap*) they hatch!

As you sing the song, take turns adding a cluster of tones on
the words *they hatch*. To play a cluster, strike a group of
bells with the edge of a small wooden ruler. Or play a
group of piano keys with your knuckles.

Will you play a cluster of high tones, or low tones?

high cluster   low cluster

Ask two friends to help you play clusters of tones on recorders.
One recorder plays G, another plays A, the third plays
B—all at the same time.

they hatch

CALL CHART 5: FORM ⊚
₅

Can you hear form in music? Listen to the recording to discover
the form of these pieces. When number 1 is called, you are
hearing section A. When you hear another number, the music
will be either a repetition of section A, or a contrast.
Follow the chart to help you hear what is happening
in the music.

---

1.   *A*
2. *CONTRAST*   *B*   Notebook for Anna Magdalena Bach, "Minuet"

---

1.   *A*
2. *CONTRAST*   *B*
3. *REPETITION*   *A*   Bichel: *Happy Moments*

---

1.   *A*
2. *REPETITION*   *A*
3. *CONTRAST*   *B*
4. *REPETITION*   *A*   Notebook for Anna Magdalena Bach, "Musette"

Create a sound piece that has three different sections. Use the tone colors and rhythm patterns shown below.

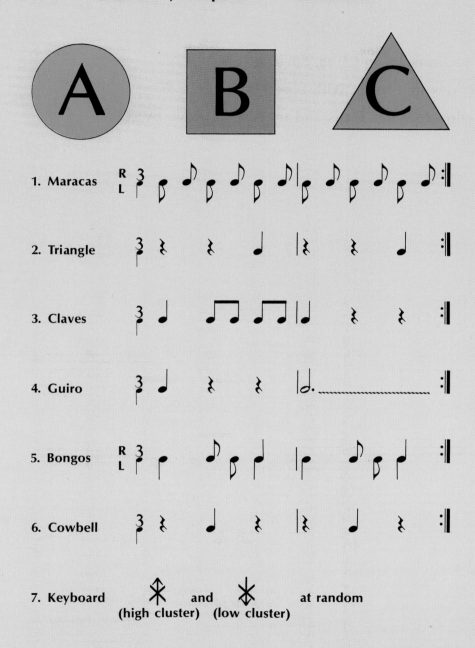

7. Keyboard ✗ and ✗ at random
   (high cluster) (low cluster)

Ways to contrast sections:

1. **Different tone colors**

2. **Different rhythm patterns**

3. **Different dynamics—p, mf, f, < >**

4. **Different tempos**

How many sections are in "Tina, Singu"?

Find the sections that begin with repeated tones.

Find the section that has leaps and tones that move by step.

TINA, SINGU   FOLK SONG FROM AFRICA

FROM CHANSONS DE NOTRE CHALET. COURTESY OF WORLD AROUND SONGS, BURNSVILLE, N.C.

Ti - na,   Sing - u,   le - lu - vu - tae - o.

Wat - sha,____   Wat - sha,____   Wat - sha.____

Wat-sha,____   Wat-sha,____   Wat-sha,____   Wat-sha,____   Wat-sha.____

La,   la - la - la - la - la - la,   la - la - la - la - la -

la,   la - la - la - la - la - la - la - la - la - la.

CALL CHART 6: FORM ◉ 5

Repetition and contrast can be used in many ways to give music form. Listen to the recording to discover how contrast is used to make version 2 of this piece different from version 1.

Following the chart will help you to hear what is going on in the music.

Kingsley: *Electronic Rondo,* Versions 1 and 2

Version 1

1.   A

2. FIRST CONTRAST   B

3. REPETITION   A

4. FIRST CONTRAST   B

5. REPETITION   A

Version 2

1.   A

2. FIRST CONTRAST   B

3. REPETITION   A

4. SECOND CONTRAST   C

5. REPETITION   A

GUAVA BERRY SONG

CHRISTMAS SONG FROM THE VIRGIN ISLANDS · ENGLISH WORDS BY JOAN GILBERT VAN POZNAK

FROM UNICEF BOOK OF CHILDREN'S SONGS, COMPILED AND WITH PHOTOGRAPHS BY WILLIAM I. KAUFMAN, COPYRIGHT 1970 BY WILLIAM I. KAUFMAN, PUBLISHED BY STACKPOLE BOOKS.

5

Come let us be joy-ful, and min-gle our song,

And hail the sweet joys which this day brings a-long.

We join our glad voic-es in one hymn of praise

To— Him— who has kept us, and—length-ened our days.

A mer-ry Christ-mas to you all, A mer-ry Christ-mas to you all,

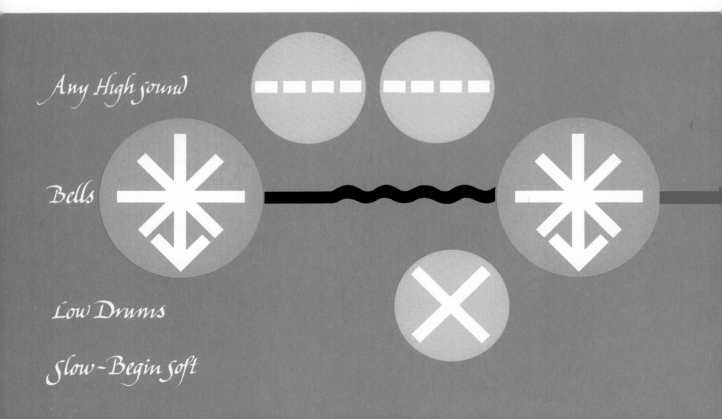

Any High sound

Bells

Low Drums

Slow~Begin soft

A mer-ry Christ-mas, A mer-ry Christ-mas, A mer-ry Christ-mas to you all!

Good morn-in', good morn-in', We wish you a mer-ry Christ-mas,

Good morn-in', good morn-in', We wish you a mer-ry Christ-mas,

Good morn-in', good morn-in', We've come for the gua-va ber-ry,

Good morn-in', good morn-in', Oh put it on the ta-ble.

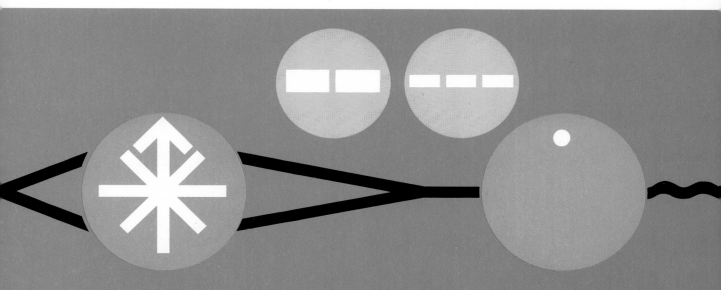

SOUND PIECE 5: Running Sound Shapes

DAVID S. WALKER

The music at the bottom of pages 106-111 in your book is written using the shapes ● and ■.

This is to show that the piece has two sections.

Where does section B begin?

Here is what the symbols in *Sound Piece 5* stand for.

LEGEND

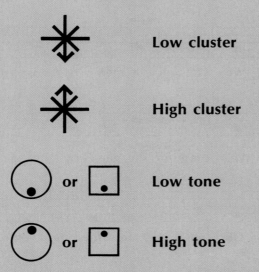

Low cluster

High cluster

or   Low tone

or   High tone

▬▬▬▬	Continue to play.
◁▷	Continue to play, getting louder.
▷◁	Continue to play, getting softer.
〜〜〜	Let the tone ring.
▬ or ✕	Play loud.
— or ✕	Play soft.

Now practice section A. While you play the bells, have one friend play the drum part, another the top part.

Another time, try section B. When your ensemble is ready to play *Sound Piece 5*, perform for the class.

Can you hear repetition and contrast in these pieces?
When number "one" is called, you will hear the
musical ideas in section A. As the other numbers are
called, decide whether the music is a repetition of A,
a first contrast of A (B), or a second contrast of A (C).

1. *A*

2. *A   B*

Purcell: *Fanfare*

---

1. *A*

2. *A   B*

3. *A   B   C*

Guava Berry Song

Fast–Begin soft

1.	*A*				
2.	*A*	*B*		**Britten:** *Scherzo* (1955)	
3.	*A*	*B*	*C*		

1.	*A*				
2.	*A*	*B*			
3.	*A*	*B*	*C*	**Tchaikovsky:** *Nutcracker Suite,* "Trepak"	
4.	*A*	*B*	*C*		

1.	*A*				
2.	*A*	*B*			
3.	*A*	*B*	*C*	**Kingsley:** *Electronic Rondo,* Version 2	
4.	*A*	*B*	*C*		
5.	*A*	*B*	*C*		

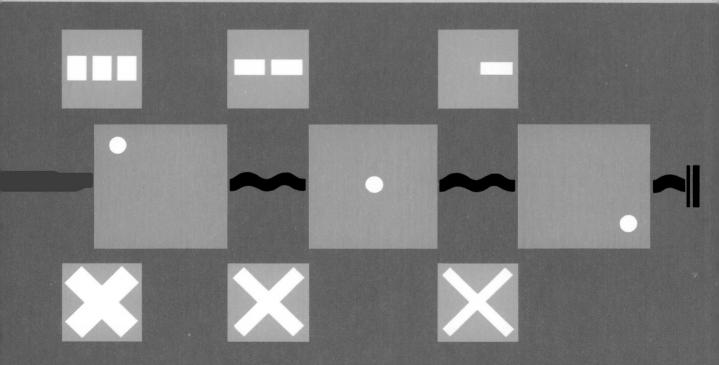

STYLE

Everything is
made of parts.

Put the parts together
and you get a "whole."

What do these numbers and colors add up to?

$$11 + 9 + 8 + 2 = 30$$

● + ● = ●

When you add the numbers, the answer is 30.

When yellow and blue are combined, the result is green.

On the recording *Combining Sounds,* you will hear the following sounds combined in two ways.

1. *LOW, SOFT SOUNDS*

2. *HIGH, LOUD SOUNDS*

3. *LONG AND SHORT SOUNDS*

4. *SOUNDS MOVING IN BOTH UPWARD AND DOWNWARD DIRECTIONS*

Do the combined sounds result in the same general sound each time?

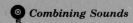 *Combining Sounds*
5

When certain numbers or colors are combined, the result is always the same.

When certain qualities of sounds are used, the combinations of sounds may result in the same style, or in different styles.

1. **Listen to this piece.**

   It uses many musical qualities—tone color, texture, etc.

   Decide what you hear for each quality listed below.

Marcello: *Sonata in F*, Movement 4

TONE COLOR	TRUMPET SAXOPHONE	FLUTE PIANO
TEXTURE	MELODY WITH HARMONY	MELODY ALONE
FORM	NO REPETITION AND CONTRAST	REPETITION AND CONTRAST
DIRECTION	UPWARD DOWNWARD	BOTH UPWARD AND DOWNWARD
DURATION	LONG SHORT	BOTH LONG AND SHORT
DYNAMICS	SOFT LOUD	BOTH SOFT AND LOUD
PHRASES	SHORT LONG	BOTH SHORT AND LONG

2. Now listen to another piece.

   It uses the same musical qualities as the first piece.

   What do you hear for each quality in this music?

Caplet: *Petite Valse*

TONE COLOR	*TRUMPET* *SAXOPHONE*	*FLUTE* *PIANO*
TEXTURE	*MELODY WITH* *HARMONY*	*MELODY* *ALONE*
FORM	*NO REPETITION* *AND CONTRAST*	*REPETITION AND* *CONTRAST*
DIRECTION	*UPWARD* *DOWNWARD*	*BOTH UPWARD* *AND DOWNWARD*
DURATION	*LONG* *SHORT*	*BOTH LONG* *AND SHORT*
DYNAMICS	*SOFT* *LOUD*	*BOTH SOFT* *AND LOUD*
PHRASES	*SHORT* *LONG*	*BOTH SHORT* *AND LONG*

REGISTER—RANGE

ISLAND HOPPING

FOLK SONG FROM GREECE   ENGLISH WORDS BY MARIA JORDAN

1. Bags are packed and all is rea - dy, can't wait ___ to

start; (can't wait ___ to start;) Boat is board-ing at the jet - ty,

soon we'll ___ de - part. (soon we'll ___ de - part.)

B G (optional harmony part)

Is - land hop - ping we ___ are ___ go - ing,

Sea is calm, a soft ___ wind's ___ blow - ing,

We can feel ex - cite - ment ___ grow - ing

in ev - 'ry heart, ___ *Ahs-toh kah-loh,* ___ In ev - 'ry ___ heart.

2. Parents with their sons and daughters planned for this day;

Now the boat glides 'cross the waters, we're on our way.

Grecian islands lie before us—

Hydra, Spetsai, lovely Poros

Beckon us as, in a chorus, "Come," they all say, *Ahstoh kahloh,*

"Come," they all say.

Play the echo in section A in a high register, or in a low register.

E C♯ B A D

Arrange the high bells like this.

Arrange the low bells like this.

To accompany "Rally Song," press the D min. chord button on the Autoharp. Use the following strumming pattern, or make up one of your own.

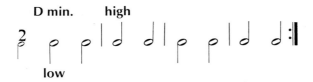

RALLY SONG

ROUND FROM THE BALKANS

FROM THE 1960 REVISED VERSION OF THE DITTY BAG BY JANET TOBITT. USED BY PERMISSION.

I

Mi ha - bi lu - lu be-shem-bel. Mi ha - bi lu - lu be-shem-bel.

II

Mi ha - bi lu - lu be-shem-bel. Mi ha - bi lu - lu be-shem-bel.

Another time, play an Autoharp accompaniment using only the strings in the middle register.

You have played in the low, middle, and high registers of the Autoharp.

Take turns accompanying "Rally Song" by playing one of these patterns on recorder or bells.

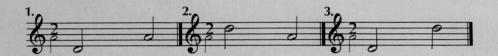

Which pattern has the widest range?

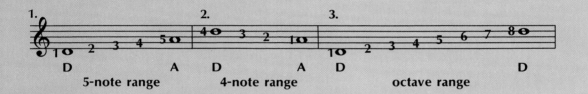

1. D ... A — 5-note range
2. D ... A — 4-note range
3. D ... D — octave range

Look at the score of "Rally Song" on p. 120. Does it have a 4-note range? A 5-note range? An octave range?

"RALLY SONG" COUNTERMELODY

Recorder or Bells

I
D   A   D

II
D   A   D

HOLD ON

AMERICAN FOLK SONG

1. Keep on plowin' and don't you tire,
   Ev'ry row goes higher and higher.
   Keep your hand on that plow,
   Hold on, hold on, hold on. *Refrain*

3. Keep on plowin' and don't you tire,
   Ev'ry row goes higher and higher.
   Keep your hand on that plow,
   Hold on, hold on, hold on. *Refrain*

4. If that plow stays in your hand,
   Head you straight for the promised land.
   Keep your hand on that plow,
   Hold on, hold on, hold on. *Refrain*

OLD BLUE

SOUTHERN MOUNTAIN SONG

A VERSE

1. I had an old dog,_____ And his name was Blue,_____

And I bet-cha five dol-lars he's a good dog, too.

B REFRAIN

Come on, Blue,_____ you good dog,_____ you;_____

Come on, Blue,_____ you good dog,_____ you._____

2. I grabbed my axe and I tooted my horn,

   Gonna git me a 'possum in the new-ground corn. *Refrain*

3. Chased that ol' 'possum up a 'simmon tree,

   Blue looked at the 'possum, 'possum looked at me. *Refrain*

4. Blue grinned at me, I grinned at him,

   I shook out the 'possum, Blue took him in. *Refrain*

5. Baked that 'possum all good and brown,

   And I laid them sweet potatoes 'round and 'round. *Refrain*

6. Well, old Blue died, and he died so hard,

   That he shook the ground in my back yard. *Refrain*

7. I dug his grave with a silver spade,

   I let him down with a golden chain. *Refrain*

8. When I get to heaven, first thing I'll do,

   Grab me a horn and blow for old Blue. *Refrain*

Stravinsky: *Greeting Prelude*

SOUND PIECE 6: Music Boxes

JOYCE BOGUSKY-REIMER   © 1980 JOYCE BOGUSKY-REIMER

Choose an instrument that makes both high and low sounds.

Then practice the events in the boxes below.

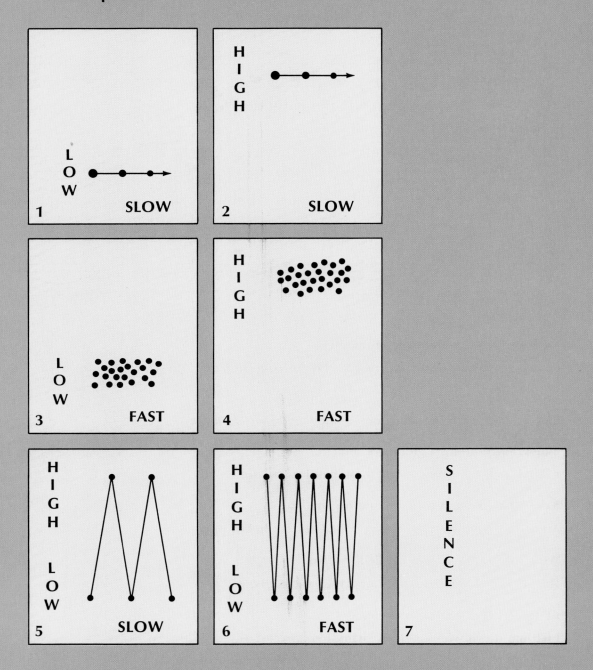

Now play the boxes in an order that gives the piece form.

You may start with any box, repeat some boxes, or omit some boxes.

On the recording, an African
performer of the Kpelle tribe
plays the triangular framed
zither. Listen for the different
registers in the music—low,
middle, high.

Zither Music

Find the lowest note and the highest note in this song.

What is the range?

SONG OF THE ANGEL

MENNONITE MELODY

© 1966 BY LAWSON-GOULD MUSIC PUBLISHERS. INC. USED BY PERMISSION

1. Fear not, fear not, good shep - herds all,

Let faith your fear de - stroy;

For lo, this night I bring to you

Good ti - dings of great joy,

Good ti - dings of great joy.

2. Awake your ears and hark to me,
   To hear the glorious Word:
   For unto you is born this day
   A Saviour, Christ the Lord,
   A Saviour, Christ the Lord.

3. You'll find the Babe in Bethlehem,
   Born of the Mary maid;
   All wrapped in swaddling clothes is He,
   And in a manger laid,
   And in a manger laid.

4. So join us now with one accord
   To sing this wondrous birth:
   Give praise to God, our heav'nly King,
   And peace to men on earth,
   And peace to men on earth.

Do these songs have a wide range, or a narrow range?

THE SEASONS OF THE YEAR

WORDS AND MUSIC BY PETER CROSSLEY-HOLLAND

Rain and sun and frost and snow;

Spring and Sum - mer, Au - tumn, Win - ter,

Round and round the sea - sons go.

Ostinato—Recorder or Bells

G A B A

FOR HEALTH AND STRENGTH

OLD ENGLISH ROUND

For health and strength and dai - ly food We praise Thy name, O Lord.

TWO LITTLE PIECES, NO. 1
ANTON BRUCKNER

FROM 44 ORIGINAL PIANO DUETS AS EDITED BY WALTER ECKARD. © 1962 THEODORE PRESSER COMPANY. USED BY PERMISSION.

WHAT DO YOU HEAR? 10: REGISTER 　◎
6

Listen to this piece. Each time a number is called, choose

the answer (or answers) that best describes the register.

Haydn: *Chorale St. Antonie*

1. HIGH REGISTER	MIDDLE REGISTER	LOW REGISTER
2. HIGH REGISTER	MIDDLE REGISTER	LOW REGISTER
3. HIGH REGISTER	MIDDLE REGISTER	LOW REGISTER
4. HIGH REGISTER	MIDDLE REGISTER	LOW REGISTER

WHAT DO YOU HEAR? 11: RANGE 　◎
6

Listen to these pieces. Each time a number is called, choose

the answer that best describes the range.

1. NARROW RANGE	WIDE RANGE	Webern: *Variations for Orchestra*
2. NARROW RANGE	WIDE RANGE	Gregorian Chant
3. NARROW RANGE	WIDE RANGE	Tchaikovsky: *The Sleeping Beauty*
4. NARROW RANGE	WIDE RANGE	*Ai a la o Pele*

THE ARTS: REPETITION WITH VARIETY AND CONTRAST

Follow the rhythm patterns below as you listen to the recording.
They will help you hear what is going on in the upper parts
of the music.

◉ Eddleman: *For Health and Strength* (*Ground with Variations*)
6

1. Ground (melody) alone

Can you see repetition as well as variety and contrast in this painting?

Use the melody of "Rally Song" as a ground. Add variety and contrast by performing one of the parts on p. 133. Use the recording of the ground while you practice your part.

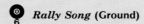 *Rally Song* (Ground)

When you and your classmates are ready, follow this arrangement as the ground repeats on the recording.

1. *ground alone*

2. *ground, bells, and Autoharp*

3.⎫
  ⎬ *ground, round, and tambourine*
4.⎭

5.⎫
  ⎬ *ground, bells, Autoharp, round, and tambourine*
6.⎭

Ground ("Rally Song") FROM THE 1960 REVISED VERSION OF THE DITTY BAG BY JANET TOBITT. USED BY PERMISSION.

Bells or Recorder

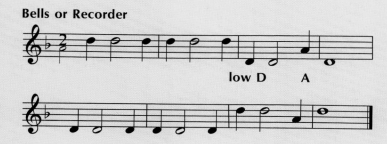

low D   A

Autoharp

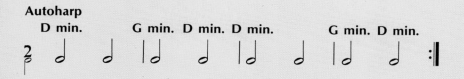

Round ("Rally Song")

Mi ha - bi lu - lu be-shem-bel. Mi ha - bi lu - lu be-shem-bel.

Mi ha - bi lu - lu be-shem-bel. Mi ha - bi lu - lu be-shem-bel.

Tambourine   (shake)

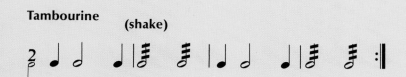

RHYTHM PATTERNS 1

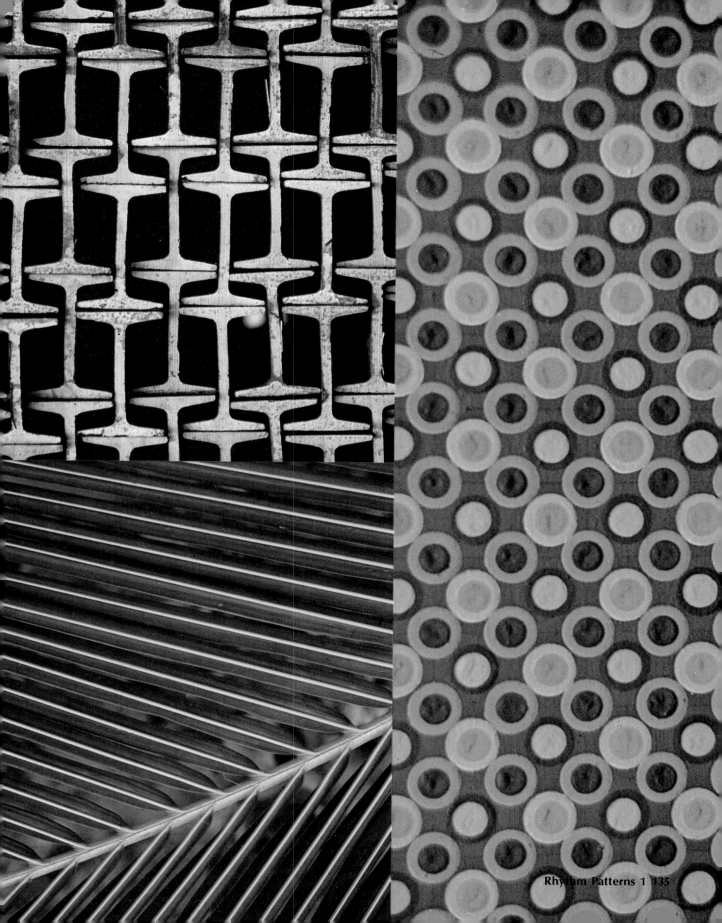

Follow the voice parts as you listen to the recording of

"Old Texas." Notice that one part sings short sounds while

the other sings long ones.

As others sing the long sounds in the melody, take turns

strumming a rhythm pattern on the Autoharp. The score will

tell you when to play the F chord and when to play

the C$_7$ chord.

OLD TEXAS OKLAHOMA COWBOY SONG

1. I'm goin' to leave_____ old__ Tex - as now,

1. I'm goin' to leave_____ old__ Tex - as now,__

They've got no use_____ for the long-horn cow._____

___ They've got no use _____ for the long-horn cow.

2. They've plowed and fenced my cattle range,
   And the people there are all so strange.

4. Say *adios* to the Alamo
   And turn my head toward Mexico.

3. I'll take my horse, I'll take my rope,
   And hit the trail upon a lope.

136 Rhythm Patterns 1

CALL CHART 7: RHYTHM PATTERNS 🔘

Listen to this piece. Each time a number is called, decide whether
you are hearing long sounds, or short sounds. Look at the chart to
check your answers.

Schumann: *Fantasiestücke*, Op. 12, No. 6, "Fable"

1. *LONG*

2. *SHORT*

3. *LONG*

4. *SHORT*

5. *SHORT*

6. *LONG*

7. *LONG*

There are many ways to combine long and short sounds and long
and short silences to make rhythm patterns.
Can you hear long and short sounds played at the same time in
this music? Strings play the long sounds. Brass instruments
play the short sounds.

🔘 Tchaikovsky: *Capriccio Italien*

Tabla are among the most popular drums of India.

1.   2.

Indian Drum Syllables

Dhe (pronounced *dhuh*)—left-hand (low) drum struck just above the middle

Na (pronounced *nah*)—right-hand (high) drum struck near the edge

Tin—right-hand drum struck near the middle

Dha (pronounced *dhah*)—*Dhe* and *Na* performed at the same time

Dhin—*Dhe* and *Tin* performed at the same time

Chant the syllables while playing this pattern on low and high drums.

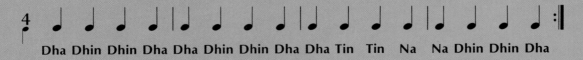

Dha Dhin Dhin Dha Dha Dhin Dhin Dha Dha Tin Tin Na Na Dhin Dhin Dha

Alla Rakha

JOY TO THE WORLD

WORDS AND MUSIC BY HOYT AXTON

1. Jer - e - mi - ah was a bull - frog, Was a good friend of mine. Nev - er un - der - stood a sin - gle word he said, but we al - ways had a might - y fine time. Yes, we al - ways had a might - y fine time.

Sing - ing joy to the world. All the boys and girls now. Joy to the fish - es in the deep blue sea. Joy to you and me.

2. If I were the king of the world, tell you what I'd do,
Throw away the fears and the tears and the jeers,
And have a good time with you.
Yes, I'd have a good time with you. *Refrain.*

Countermelody

Sing - ing joy to the world, Joy to the world;

Joy, joy, joy, joy, Joy to you and me.

Fill in the silences in the melody with a pattern of long and short sounds.

NAUGHTY LITTLE FLEA

WORDS AND MUSIC BY NORMAN THOMAS

TRANSCRIBED FROM THE RECORDING BY MIRIAM MAKEBA AND HARRY BELAFONTE

© 1957 PINEBROOK MUSIC CORP. c/o H/B WEBMAN & COMPANY. USED BY PERMISSION.

Where did the naught-y lit - tle flea go?
Won't some-bod - y tell me? Where did the naught-y lit - tle
flea go? Won't some - bod - y tell me?
1. There was a naught - y lit - tle flea; He climbed up on the
dog - gie's knee; He climbed some here, he climbed some there;
He was climb - ing ev - 'ry - where. Tell me,

2. He climbed some here,
    he climbed some there;
He was climbing everywhere.
And now at last he's found a nest
Where he can get some food and rest.
Tell me, . . .

3. He bit him here,
    he bit him there;
He bit him almost everywhere.
When he was done he wanted more;
He never tasted such a dog before.
Tell me, . . .

Listen for the rhythm pattern when the vowels are chanted in *A-E-I-O-U*.

 A-E-I-O-U

Listen to these pieces. Do you hear mostly short sounds, mostly
long sounds, or short and long sounds together? Each time
a number is called, decide which of the three answers is
correct. Choose the answer that best describes what is
happening in the music.

1. MOSTLY SHORT   MOSTLY LONG   SHORT AND LONG TOGETHER   Stockhausen: *Klavierstück*

2. MOSTLY SHORT   MOSTLY LONG   SHORT AND LONG TOGETHER   Mendelssohn: *Nocturne*

3. MOSTLY SHORT   MOSTLY LONG   SHORT AND LONG TOGETHER   Tchaikovsky: *Capriccio Italien*

4. MOSTLY SHORT   MOSTLY LONG   SHORT AND LONG TOGETHER   Vivaldi: *The Four Seasons,* "Winter"

5. MOSTLY SHORT   MOSTLY LONG   SHORT AND LONG TOGETHER   *Goin' down the Road Feeling Bad*

RHYTHM PATTERNS 2

Notice the triplet ♪♪♪ in each phrase as you sing this song.

How many triplets can you find?

THE MOSQUITO

FOLK SONG FROM COLOMBIA   ENGLISH WORDS BY MARGARET MARKS

1. I went to the Sie-rra Blan-ca   To hunt with my dog, Pe-rri-to,

When sud-den-ly I en-count-ered   a great o-ver-grown mos-qui-to.

I dropped to my knees and fired,__   And star-tled by that ex-plo-sion,

The an-i-mal lost his bal-ance   And tum-bled in-to the o-cean.

2. So huge was this big mosquito,
   A tidal wave swelled the water,
   His head lay in Cádiz harbor,
   His feet lay across Gibraltar.
   And then the ordeal was over,
   The bug ceased to make a motion,
   I called for a crane and derrick,
   You've never seen such commotion.

3. They made from his hide ten thousand
   High boots of the finest leather,
   And just from the bits left over,
   A hundred or so umbrellas;
   And even now, ten years later,
   Though nothing could seem absurder,
   The whole of the Spanish Army
   Is eating mosquito-burger!

Can you hear triplets in this piece for piano?

Mozart: *Variations on "Ah, vous dirai-je, Maman?"*

Find the triplets in this music.

DIN, DON FOLK MELODY FROM SPAIN

MUSICAL SETTING FROM THE BABY'S SONG BOOK © 1971 ELIZABETH POSTON. USED BY PERMISSION OF THOMAS Y. CROWELL AND THE BODLEY HEAD.

Percussion Parts

Wood Block

Finger Cymbals

Tap the rhythm of the melody. On which words do you tap the shortest sounds?

KOOKABURRA

WORDS AND MUSIC BY MARION SINCLAIR

FROM THE DITTY BAG, COMPILED BY JANET E. TOBITT. USED WITH PERMISSION.

I

Kook - a - bur - ra   sits   on   the   old   gum   tree,____

II

Mer - ry,   mer - ry   king   of   the   bush   is   he,____

III   IV

Laugh, kook - a - bur - ra, laugh, kook - a - bur - ra, Gay   your   life   must   be.

Choose one of these rhythm patterns to play on a percussion instrument throughout "Kookaburra."

SOUND PIECE 7: Intersections

DAVID S. WALKER

Each vertical column in the score stands for one beat.

Follow the red, green, or purple line to see where the beat is divided. Is the beat divided into two, three, or four sounds?

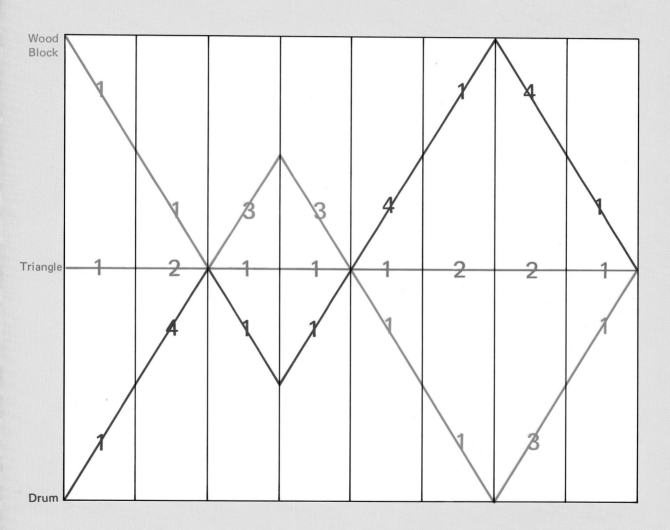

Choose one of the parts to play. Team up with two others to perform your version of *Sound Piece 7*.

TA-RA-RA BOOM-DE-AY

WORDS AND MUSIC BY HENRY SAYERS

Ta - ra - ra boom - de - ay,   Ta - ra - ra boom - de - ay,

Ta - ra - ra boom - de - ay,   Ta - ra - ra boom - de - ay,

Ta - ra - ra boom - de - ay,   Ta - ra - ra boom - de - ay,

Ta - ra - ra boom - de - ay,   Ta - ra - ra boom - de - ay._____

Practice this new tone on recorder.

Then play the part that follows

as others sing the song.

Be sure to play dotted rhythms.

F#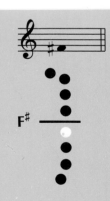

Recorder or Bells

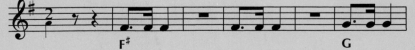

F#   G

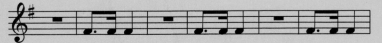

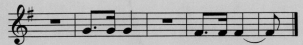

RED, RED ROBIN

WORDS AND MUSIC BY HARRY WOODS

When the red, red rob-in comes bob, bob, bob-bin' a-long, a-long, There'll be no more sob-bin' when he starts throb-bin' his old sweet song. "Wake up, wake up, you sleep-y head! Get up, get up, get out of bed; Cheer up, cheer up, the sun is red; Live, love, laugh and be hap-py!" What if I've been blue, now I'm walk-in' through fields of flowers; Rain may glis-ten but still I'll lis-ten for hours and hours. I'm just a kid a-gain, do-in' what I did a-gain, Sing-ing a song, When the red, red rob-in comes bob, bob, bob-bin' a-long.

Here is part of a song you know written two ways.

How are the patterns alike? How are they different?

1.

Do,___ Lord, O do,___ Lord, O

2.

Do, Lord,___ O do, Lord, ___ O

Find the syncopation in this song.

LET THE SUN SHINE DOWN ON ME

WORDS AND MUSIC BY 'THAN HALL

REFRAIN D MIN. D MIN.

O, roll on, clouds in the morn - in', Roll on, clouds in the

C D MIN. D MIN.

morn - in';___ Roll on, clouds in the morn - in', Let the

D MIN. C D MIN. *Fine* D MIN.

sun shine down on me. 1. I looked out this morn - in', _____
2. I know there's a great day com - in', When

D MIN. D MIN.

Deep - down trou - ble I see; Yes, I looked out this
no more trou - ble I see; When we'll all shout to -

D.C. al Fine

D MIN. D MIN. C D MIN.

morn - in', Let the sun shine down on me.
geth - er, Let the sun shine down on me.

TINGA LAYO

CALYPSO FROM THE WEST INDIES   ENGLISH VERSION BY MARGARET MARKS

Tin - ga Lay - o!   Run, lit - tle don - key, run!
¡Ven, mi bu - rri - to, ven!

1.-3.   *Last time only*

Tin - ga Lay - o!   Run, lit - tle don - key, run! run!
¡Ven, mi bu - rri - to, ven! ven!

1. My don - key yes, my don - key no,
1. *Bu - rri - to sí, bu - rri - to no.*

My don - key stop when I tell him to go!
¡Bu - rri - to co - me con te - ne - dor!

2. My donkey hee, my donkey haw,
   My donkey sit on the kitchen floor! *Refrain*

3. My donkey kick, my donkey balk,
   My donkey eat with a silver fork! *Refrain*

Play one of these patterns throughout the song.

Which one uses syncopation?

1. (steady beat)

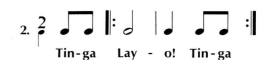

2. Tin - ga Lay - o! Tin - ga

3. Run, lit - tle don-key, run!

Feel the syncopation every time you sing the phrase *See, can't you jump for joy.*

SEE, CAN'T YOU JUMP FOR JOY

BLACK-AMERICAN RING SHOUT

My Lord calls me, See, can't you jump for joy,_____

See, can't you jump for joy,_____

See, can't you jump for joy._____

My Lord calls me, See, can't you jump for joy,_____

Broth-er, can't you jump for joy._____

Do a stamp-clap pattern as you sing the song.

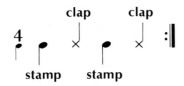

Listen to this song. In which section can you feel syncopation?

Does the melody of each section sound as it looks in the notation?

GRANDPA
WORDS AND MUSIC BY CHRIS DEDRICK   © 1972 ALMITRA MUSIC COMPANY, INC.

(A) VERSE

1. Grand - pa is a qui - et name for a ver - y qui - et man.
2. Get to know your grand - pa, you can___ learn a lot from him.

And no one else re - mem - bers all the things that Grand - pa can.
His know - ledge has a beau - ty like the leaves up - on a limb.

Sto - ries full of truth - ful - ness that time can - not e - rase
Like the leaf, a pat - tern,___ and like the branch, a strength,

Are writ - ten out like gos - pel in the wrin - kles of his face.
For, like the tree, he's breathed the wind and watched the world at length.

[B] REFRAIN*

Grand - pa, Grand - pa - pa, ___   Grand - pa - pa - pa, ___

Grand - pa - pa - pa - pa. _____

Repeat refrain last time.

3. Sometimes you can sit with him and never say a word.

    You start to think of silence as a sound that can be heard,

    And, hearing it, you're led into a diff'rent place to live

    Where nothing scares or hurts you, and there's nothing to forgive.

WHAT DO YOU HEAR? 13: RHYTHM PATTERNS 🎵

Listen to these pieces. Do you hear syncopation, or no syncopation?
Each time a number is called, decide which of the two answers is
correct. Choose the answer that best describes what is happening
in the music.

---

1. *SYNCOPATION   NO SYNCOPATION*   Joplin: *The Entertainer*

---

2. *SYNCOPATION   NO SYNCOPATION*   Hays: *Arabella Rag*

---

3. *SYNCOPATION   NO SYNCOPATION*   Handel: *Sonata in F*

---

4. *SYNCOPATION   NO SYNCOPATION*   Debussy: *Golliwog's Cake Walk*

---

5. *SYNCOPATION   NO SYNCOPATION*   *Find the Ring*

---

6. *SYNCOPATION   NO SYNCOPATION*   Malinke Tribe: *Drum Duet*

"America, the Beautiful" Countermelody

Recorder or Bells

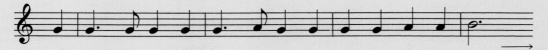

Notice that each phrase of "America, the Beautiful" uses the same rhythm pattern.

AMERICA, THE BEAUTIFUL

MUSIC BY SAMUEL A. WARD   WORDS BY KATHARINE LEE BATES

O beau - ti - ful   for spa - cious skies, For am - ber waves of grain,
O beau - ti - ful   for pa - triot dream That sees be - yond the years

For pur - ple moun - tain maj - es - ties   A - bove the fruit - ed   plain!
Thine al - a - bas - ter cit - ies gleam, Un-dimmed by hu - man tears!

A - mer - i - ca!   A - mer - i - ca!   God shed His grace on   thee

And crown   thy good with broth - er - hood From sea   to shin - ing sea!

CLEMENTINE

AMERICAN FOLK SONG

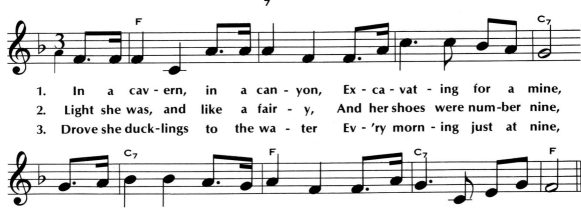

1. In a cav - ern, in a can - yon, Ex - ca - vat - ing for a mine,
2. Light she was, and like a fair - y, And her shoes were num - ber nine,
3. Drove she duck - lings to the wa - ter Ev - 'ry morn - ing just at nine,

Dwelt a min - er, for - ty - nin - er, And his daugh - ter, Clem - en - tine.
Her - ring box - es with - out top - ses, San - dals were for Clem - en - tine.
Hit her foot a - gainst a splin - ter, Fell in - to the foam - ing brine.

REFRAIN

(optional harmony part)

Oh, my dar - ling, oh, my dar - ling, Oh, my dar - ling Clem - en - tine,

You are lost and gone for - ev - er, Dread - ful sor - ry, Clem - en - tine.

Play these rhythm patterns to accompany "Clementine."

Sticks (Play four times.)

Tambourine (Play four times.) (shake)

Autoharp

WHAT DO YOU HEAR? 14: RHYTHM PATTERNS

Listen to these pieces. Each time a number is called, decide which pattern you are hearing.

1. The Mosquito

2. Mozart: *Symphony No. 40*

3. *America, the Beautiful*

4. Haydn: *String Quartet, Op. 76*

5. Tchaikovsky: *Symphony No. 6*

6. Beethoven: *Symphony No. 7*

What do these drawings show?

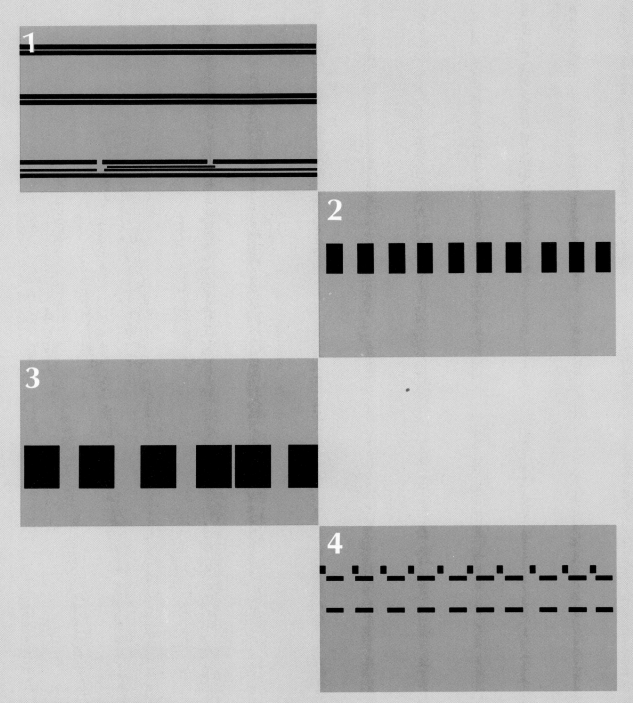

This rhythm pattern is from a song that you know.

Can you name the song?

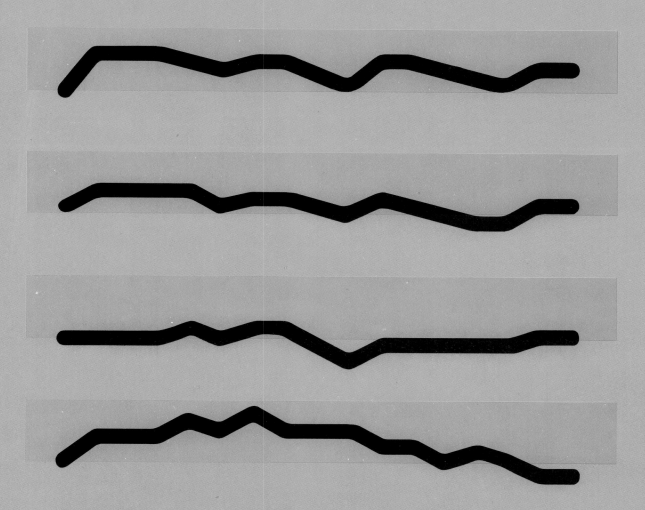

What do these lines show?

A painting can have pattern, line, direction. Can a piece of music have pattern, line, and direction also?

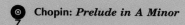 Chopin: *Prelude in A Minor*

TONE COLOR
VOICES

In the recording of *Swing Low, Sweet Chariot,* you hear both women's and men's voices.

 Swing Low, Sweet Chariot

ALL HID

TRADITIONAL

Use the tone color of your natural speaking voice when
you read this poem.

Windy winter rain . . .
My silly big umbrella
Tries walking backward.

Shisei-Jo

Now look at the notation for the Sound Piece on p. 163. Notice that
the score uses symbols to stand for different voice sounds. The
legend below tells what the symbols mean.

LEGEND

Ͼ   Blow.

Φ   Whistle.

♪   Whisper.

∞   Make the sound continue.

▯▯▯▯   Make unvoiced lip and mouth sounds
        without breathing out.

SOUND PIECE 8: Windy Winter Rain ALLEN BRINGS

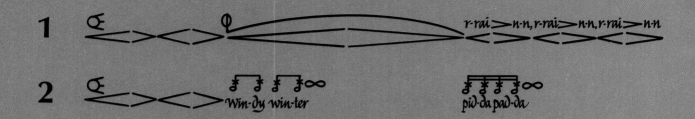

1   r-rai > n-n, r-rai > n-n, r-rai > n-n

2   Win-dy win-ter   pid-da pad-da

1   My sil-ly big um-brel--la

2   My sil-ly, sil-ly big al-lerb-mu

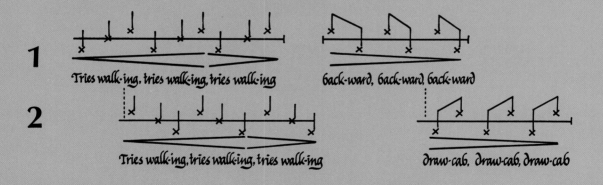

1   Tries walk-ing, tries walk-ing, tries walk-ing   back-ward, back-ward, back-ward

2   Tries walk-ing, tries walk-ing, tries walk-ing   draw-cab, draw-cab, draw-cab

1

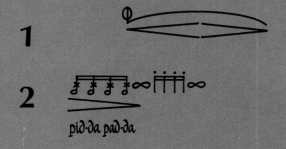

2   pid-da pad-da

Read the lyrics to learn the story of Don Gato. Then sing the song.

A song that tells a story is called a ballad.

DON GATO

FOLK SONG FROM MEXICO   ENGLISH WORDS BY MARGARET MARKS

1. Oh, Se - ñor Don Ga - to was a cat,_____
2. "I a - dore you!" wrote the la - dy cat,_____

On a high, red roof Don Ga - to sat._____
Who was fluff - y, white, and nice and fat._____

He went there to read a let - ter, meow, meow, meow,
There was not a sweet - er kit - ty,

Where the read - ing light was bet - ter, meow, meow, meow,
In the coun - try or the cit - y,

'Twas a love note for Don Ga - to!_____
And she said she'd wed Don Ga - to!_____

3. Oh, Don Gato jumped so happily
   He fell off the roof and broke his knee,
   Broke his ribs and all his whiskers, . . .
   And his little solar plexus, . . .
   "¡Ay carramba!" cried Don Gato!

4. Then the doctors all came on the run
   Just to see if something could be done,
   And they held a consultation, . . .
   About how to save their patient, . . .
   How to save Señor Don Gato!

5. But in spite of everything they tried
   Poor Señor Don Gato up and died,
   Oh, it wasn't very merry, . . .
   Going to the cemetery, . . .
   For the ending of Don Gato!

6. When the funeral passed the market square
   Such a smell of fish was in the air,
   Though his burial was slated, . . .
   He became re-animated! . . .
   He came back to life, Don Gato!

Decide on a sound effect for each of these symbols. Add the sound effects when you sing "Don Gato."

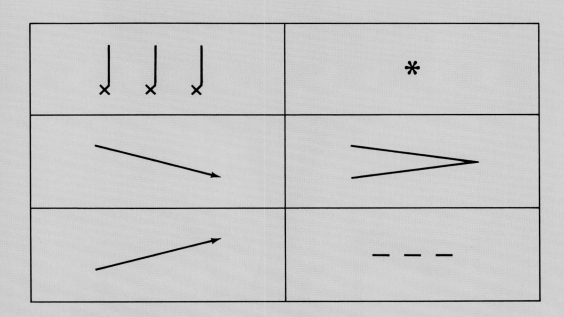

PERCUSSION INSTRUMENTS

Listen to an ensemble of percussion instruments in this recording.

McKenzie: *Samba*

You have played percussion instruments to accompany many songs that you know. Decide on a song, then choose a percussion instrument to play while the class sings along.

Think of a way to accompany this song on percussion instruments.

Which tone colors will you use?

SHE'LL BE COMIN' ROUND THE MOUNTAIN

SOUTHERN MOUNTAIN SONG

1. She'll be com - in' round the moun - tain when she comes,_____
2. She'll be driv - in' six white hor - ses when she comes,_____

She'll be com - in' round the moun - tain when she comes,_____
She'll be driv - in' six white hor - ses when she comes,_____

She'll be com - in' round the moun - tain,
She'll be driv - in' six white hor - ses,

She'll be com - in' round the moun - tain,
She'll be driv - in' six white hor - ses,

She'll be com - in' round the moun - tain when she comes._____
She'll be driv - in' six white hor - ses when she comes._____

3. Oh, we'll kill the old red rooster when she comes, . . .

4. Oh, we'll all have chicken and dumplings when she comes, . . .

5. Oh, we'll all go out to meet her when she comes, . . .

Follow the chord names in the music to play an accompaniment on the Autoharp. You will use the chords G, D$_7$, C.

Play these percussion parts to accompany "Hotsia!"

In each part, silently say the numbers in time with the steady beat.

Play the instrument whenever you say a large-size number.

Cowbell

1 2 3 4 5 6 7 8 9 10 11 12

High Drum

1 2 3 4 5 6 7 8 9 10 11 12

Rattle

1 2 3 4 5 6 7 8 9 10 11 12

HOTSIA!

VENDA CHILDREN'S SONG   ENGLISH WORDS BY RICHARD MORRIS

THIS IS A FREE TRANSLATION OF A VERY SIMPLE CHILDREN'S SONG. ORIGINALLY PUBLISHED AS "HOTSIA" IN J. A. R. BLACKING. VENDA CHILDREN'S SONGS
(JOHANNESBURG, WITWATERSRAND UNIVERSITY PRESS, 1967), P. 108, AND REPRODUCED HERE WITH THE PERMISSION OF THE WITWATERSRAND UNIVERSITY PRESS AND OF THE AUTHOR.

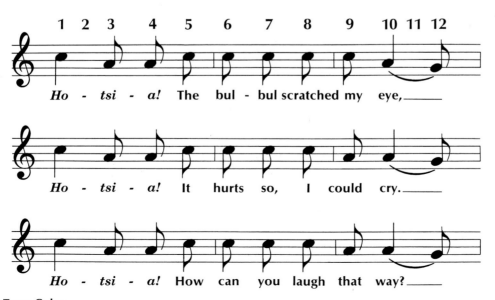

Ho - tsi - a! The bul - bul scratched my eye,_____

Ho - tsi - a! It hurts so, I could cry._____

Ho - tsi - a! How can you laugh that way?_____

Ho - tsi - a! You're not my friend to - day.____

Ho - tsi - a! Oh, did - n't we have fun? ____

Ho - tsi - a! How those ba - boons did run____

Ho - tsi - a! From old Ne - khum - be's gar - den,

Ho - tsi - a! When we all yelled and chased them

Ho - tsi - a! Back up in - to the moun - tains.

The word *hotsia* means "sneeze." In Africa, this sound is supposed
to frighten away birds, baboons, and other pests that eat
the crops.

AUTOHARP

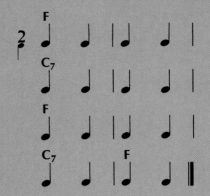

SKIP TO MY LOU   AMERICAN GAME SONG

1. <u>Flies</u> in the buttermilk, shoo, fly, shoo!
   Flies in the buttermilk, shoo, fly, shoo!
   Flies in the buttermilk, shoo, fly, shoo!
   Skip to my Lou, my darling.

2. Little red wagon painted blue,

3. Lost my partner, what'll I do?

4. I'll get another, better than you!

BILLY BOY   FOLK SONG FROM ENGLAND

1. Oh, <u>where</u> have you been, Billy Boy, Billy Boy?
   Oh, where have you been, charming Billy?
   I have been to seek a wife,
   She's the joy of my life,
   She's a young thing and cannot leave her mother.

2. Did she bid you to come in, Billy Boy, Billy Boy?
   Did she bid you to come in, charming Billy?
   Yes, she bid me to come in,
   There's a dimple in her chin,
   She's a young thing and cannot leave her mother.

3. Did she give you a chair, Billy Boy, Billy Boy?
   Yes, she gave me a chair,
   But there was no bottom there . . .

4. Can she make a cherry pie, Billy Boy, Billy Boy?
   She can make a cherry pie,
   Quick as a cat can wink her eye . . .

5. Can she cook and can she spin, Billy Boy, Billy Boy?
   She can cook and she can spin,
   She can do most anything . . .

6. How old is she, Billy Boy, Billy Boy?
   Three times six and four times seven,
   Twenty-eight and eleven . . .

POLLY WOLLY DOODLE

AMERICAN FOLK SONG

1. Oh, I <u>went</u> down South for to see my Sal,
   Singing Polly Wolly Doodle all the day;
   My Sal, she is a spunky gal,
   Singing Polly Wolly Doodle all the day.

Refrain
   Fare thee well, fare thee well,
   Fare thee well my fairy fay,
   For I'm goin' to Louisiana, for to see my Susyanna,
   Singing Polly Wolly Doodle all the day.

2. Oh, my Sal, she is a maiden fair,
   Singing Polly Wolly Doodle all the day;
   With curly eyes and laughing hair,
   Singing Polly Wolly Doodle all the day.

3. The partridge is a pretty bird,
   It has a speckled breast,
   It steals away the farmer's grain,
   And totes it to its nest!

4. The raccoon's tail is ringed around,
   The 'possum's tail is bare,
   The rabbit's got no tail at all,
   Just a little bitty bunch of hair!

5. The June-bug he has golden wings,
   The lightning bug totes a flame,
   The caterpillar's got no wings at all,
   But he gets there just the same!

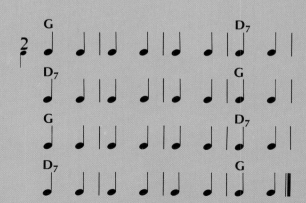

AIN'T GONNA RAIN

AMERICAN FOLK SONG

1. The <u>wood</u>chuck, he's a-choppin' wood,
   The 'possum, he's a-haulin'.
   My poor old dog fell off a log
   And killed himself a-bawlin'.

Refrain
   It ain't gonna rain, it ain't gonna rain,
   It ain't gonna rain no more.
   Come on down, ev'rybody sing.
   It ain't gonna rain no more.

2. Just bake them biscuits good and brown,
   It ain't gonna rain no more.
   Swing your ladies round and round,
   It ain't gonna rain no more.

3. I'll tune the fiddle, you get the bow,
   It ain't gonna rain no more.
   The weatherman just told me so,
   It ain't gonna rain no more.

4. Oh, what did the blackbird say to the crow?
   "It ain't gonna rain no more.
   It ain't gonna hail, it ain't gonna snow,
   It ain't gonna rain no more."

Tone Color 171

RECORDERS

Soprano

Alto

Tenor

Bass

Listen to a soprano recorder as it plays in a consort, or group. The soprano recorder plays in a higher register than the alto, tenor, and bass recorders.

In Dulci Jubilo

The soprano recorder part you heard is notated below. Practice the part so you can play along with the recording. You will need a new tone, high E.

E

IN DULCI JUBILO
GERMAN MELODY

BRASS INSTRUMENTS

You have heard the tone color of recorders playing in an ensemble. The tone colors of brass instruments can be combined in an ensemble also. Listen to this music for brass ensemble.

🎵 M. Franck: *Intrada II*
8

Trombones

Trumpets

AMERICA

TRADITIONAL MELODY   WORDS BY SAMUEL FRANCIS SMITH

My coun - try! 'tis   of thee, Sweet land   of   lib - er - ty,
Our   fa - thers' God,   to Thee, Au - thor   of   lib - er - ty,

Of thee   I   sing;   Land where   my   fa - thers died,
To Thee we sing;   Long may   our   land   be bright

Land   of the Pil - grim's pride, From   ev - 'ry ___ moun - tain - side
With free - dom's ho - ly light; Pro - tect ___ us ___ by   Thy might,

Let ___ free - dom ring!
Great __ God, our King!

If you play trumpet, practice the part below. Then play along with
the brass ensemble on the recording as others sing "America."

Trumpet

WOODWIND QUINTET

Flute

Listen to the tone color of a woodwind quintet.
The picture shows the instruments
that make up the ensemble.

 Ibert: *Trois pièces brèves,* No. 3

If you play the clarinet or flute,
practice the parts for "America"
to play for the class.

AMERICA   TRADITIONAL

Clarinet

Oboe

French Horn

Clarinet

Bassoon

Countermelody

Flute

STRING INSTRUMENTS

Violins

Viola

Cello

 Mozart: *String Quartet in D Minor*

THE FROG IN THE WELL

FOLK SONG FROM THE SOUTHERN APPALACHIANS

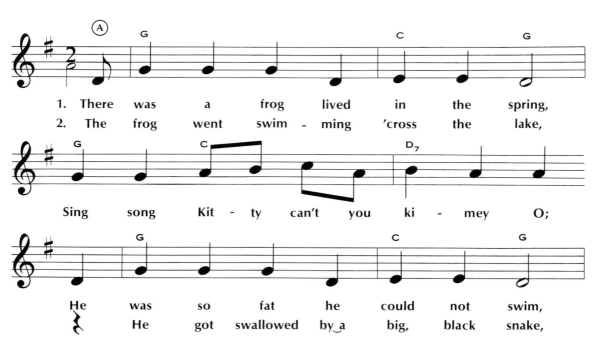

1. There was a frog lived in the spring,
2. The frog went swim - ming 'cross the lake,

Sing song Kit - ty can't you ki - mey O;

He was so fat he could not swim,
He got swallowed by a big, black snake,

178 Tone Color

Sing song Kit - ty can't you ki - mey O.

Kee - mey O ma ki - mey O ma dir - ey O ma wear,

Me hi, me ho, me in come Sal - ly Sin - gle,

Some time Pen-ny Win-kle, In stepped nip cat, Hit him with a brick bat,

Sing song Kit - ty can't you ki - mey O.

If you play violin, add its tone color to section A of "The Frog in the Well." Choose one of the parts below to play. Will you bow the strings, or pluck them?

Section A

1.

Section A

2.

KEYBOARD INSTRUMENTS

Listen to two keyboard instruments
playing the same piece.
Neither instrument is the piano.
Are the tone colors of the two
instruments the same, or different?

 Clarke (Purcell): *Trumpet Tune*
8

Harpsichord

Piano

Pipe Organ

ELECTRONIC INSTRUMENTS

Composers have always been fascinated by new possibilities for sounds. They are always looking for new ways to produce sounds and new ways to put sounds together.

Synthesizer

Amplified Guitar

Electronic Old Blue

WHAT DO YOU HEAR? 15: TONE COLOR 🔘

Can you hear tone color in music?

Listen to these pieces. Each time a number is called,

decide which answer

is correct.

Listen. Then choose

your answer.

1. PERCUSSION
VOICES
KEYBOARD
RECORDERS
BRASS
STRINGS
WOODWINDS

Five Villancicos, No. 4

2. PERCUSSION
VOICES
KEYBOARD
RECORDERS
BRASS
STRINGS
WOODWINDS

For the Beauty of the Earth

3. PERCUSSION
VOICES
KEYBOARD
RECORDERS
BRASS
STRINGS
WOODWINDS

Webern: *Five Movements
for String Quartet, Op. 5, No. 3*

4. PERCUSSION
VOICES
KEYBOARD
RECORDERS
BRASS
STRINGS
WOODWINDS

Joplin: *The Entertainer*

5. PERCUSSION
VOICES
KEYBOARD
RECORDERS
BRASS
STRINGS
WOODWINDS

McKenzie: *Three Dances, "Samba"*

6. PERCUSSION
VOICES
KEYBOARD
RECORDERS
BRASS
STRINGS
WOODWINDS

Bach: *Fugue in G Minor*

7. PERCUSSION
VOICES
KEYBOARD
RECORDERS
BRASS
STRINGS
WOODWINDS

Locke: *Courante*

8. PERCUSSION
VOICES
KEYBOARD
RECORDERS
BRASS
STRINGS
WOODWINDS

Pierne: *Pastorale*

Boys and girls in Puerto Rico play percussion instruments to
accompany Christmas carols. Use maracas, bongos, and claves
and create your own percussion parts. Then play along with
the recording.

HURRY, GOOD SHEPHERDS

Pastores a Belén

CHRISTMAS SONG FROM PUERTO RICO

ENGLISH VERSION BY VERNE MUÑOZ

Oh, hur - ry on your way;___ Good shep - herds, hur - ry to see Him.
Pas - to - res, a Be - lén___ Va - mos con a - le - grí - a;

The Son of Mar - y waits;___ Good shep - herds, hur - ry to greet Him.
Que ha na - ci - do ya___ El Hi - jo de___ Ma - rí - a.

In Beth - le - hem,___ the bless - ed Ba - by lies.___
A - llí,___ a - llí,___ Nos es - pe - ra Je - sús.___

In Beth - le - hem,___ the bless - ed Ba - by lies.___
A - llí,___ a - llí,___ Nos es - pe - ra Je - sús.___

Bring hon - ey sweet for Mar - y's Son, And al - mond cakes for ev - 'ry - one.
Lle - ve - mos pues tu - rro - nes y miel Pa - ra o - fre - cer al Ni - ño Man - uel,

Bring hon - ey sweet for Mar - y's Son, And al - mond cakes for ev - 'ry - one.
Lle - ve - mos pues tu - rro - nes y miel Pa - ra o - fre - cer al Ni - ño Man - uel.

Hur - ry, hur - ry, do not de - lay, Greet___ the Ba - by born___ this day,___
Va - mos, va - mos, va - mos a ver, Va - mos a ver al re - cién na - ci - do,

Greet___ the Ba - by born___ this day.
Va - mos a ver al Ni - ño Man - uel.

Play these percussion parts to accompany "Purim Song."

Grager

Tambourine Grager   Tambourine Grager

Grager

PURIM SONG

HASIDIC FOLK MELODY   ENGLISH WORDS BY ELIZABETH S. BACHMAN

Come a - long, come a - long, Sing a mer - ry Pu - rim song.

Cel - e - brate, cel - e - brate, Joy - ous hol - i - day.

Come, twirl the gra - ger round and round; Let's fill the room with hap - py sound;

Now pass the ha - man - tash - en round; Joy - ous hol - i - day.

STYLE: JAZZ

Here are some musical qualities that are used in the style called *Jazz*.

LOUD   *SOFT*
FAST   *SLOW*
BIG BAND *SMALL COMBO*

　　　IMPROVISATION

Listen to these jazz pieces. For each one, decide which qualities you hear.

🔘 Lewis and Gillespie: *Two Bass Hit*
8

🔘 Kern: *Yesterdays*
8

🔘 Selden: *The Magic Bus Ate My Doughnut*
8

CALL CHART 8: JAZZ

Listen to the recording. As each number is called, look at the chart. It will help you to hear what is going on in the music.

Olson and Staton: *All I Recall is You*

1. *SOFT, MODERATE TEMPO, PIANO IMPROVISES*

2. *BIG BAND ENTERS, GETS LOUDER*

3. *BASS INSTRUMENT IMPROVISES—BAND ACCOMPANIES*

4. *SAXOPHONE IMPROVISES, GETS SOFTER*

5. *DRUM IMPROVISES*

6. *BIG BAND ENTERS, GETS LOUDER*

7. *GETS SOFTER, THEN LOUDER*

8. *ENDS SOFT*

MELODY

Play these bell patterns to accompany "Evening." Which one has tones that leap?

Tones that repeat? Tones that move by step?

1. D E F G A

2. low D high D

3. A

EVENING

FOLK MELODY FROM HUNGARY   ENGLISH WORDS BY ROSEMARY JACQUES

Voic - es fill the eve - ning air with their hap - py sing - ing,

Joy and laugh-ter ev - 'ry-where through the land are ring - ing.

Cast - ing all their cares a - way, Danc - ers whirl till

break of day. Hear the mu - sic play.

Voic - es fill the eve - ning air with their hap - py sing - ing,

Joy and laugh-ter ev - 'ry-where through the land are ring - ing.

Melody 189

A melody can have tones that move upward or downward by step, tones that leap, and tones that repeat. The way the tones move gives the melody a shape, or contour.

Look at the contour of each phrase in this song. Which phrases have repeated tones?

ROOKOOMBINE FOLK SONG FROM JAMAICA

MELODY AND WORDS OF FIRST VERSE FROM FOLK SONGS OF JAMAICA, EDITED AND ARRANGED BY TOM MURRAY. COPYRIGHT 1952 BY THE OXFORD UNIVERSITY PRESS, LONDON; WORDS OF SECOND VERSE FROM FOLK SONGS OF THE CARIBBEAN BY JIM MORSE. COPYRIGHT © 1958 BY BANTAM BOOKS. USED BY PERMISSION.

1. Train top a bridge jus - a run like a breeze,
2. Went King - ston town just to have me look a - roun',

An' a gal un - der - neath it a wash her che - mise.
But in - stead look a - roun', oh, me spent ev - 'ry poun'.

B REFRAIN

Oh, Roo - koom - bine ee - na San - ta Fe,

Roo-koom - bine ee - na San - ta Fe, Oh, Roo-koom - bine. ___

Here is a bell part to play during section A of "Rookoombine."

Bells

C Bb A G

To play a recorder part with
"Rookoombine," you need
a new tone—B♭.

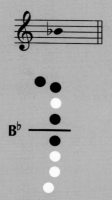

B♭

Now play this recorder part. Will you play any tones that leap?

Recorder or Bells

Do the tones in this melody move mostly by leap, by step, or do they repeat? Follow the notation as you listen to the recording.

AMAZING GRACE
EARLY AMERICAN MELODY   WORDS BY JOHN NEWTON

1. A - maz - ing____ grace   how   sweet   the   sound

That   saved   a____ wretch   like   me!_____

I   once____ was____ lost,   but   now____ am____ found,

Was   blind,   but____ now   I   see._____

2. 'Twas grace that taught my heart to fear,
   And grace my fears relieved;
   How precious did that grace appear
   The hour I first believed!

3. Through many dangers, toils, and snares,
   I have already come;
   'Tis grace has brought me safe thus far,
   And grace will lead me home.

4. The Lord has promised good to me,
   His word my hope secures;
   He will my shield and portion be
   As long as life endures.

Listen for tones that step,
leap, and repeat in
the dulcimer part
on the recording.
Listen for the many
repeated sounds in
the accompaniment
for verse 4.

Find the steps, leaps, and repeated tones in "Chopsticks."

CHOPSTICKS TRADITIONAL

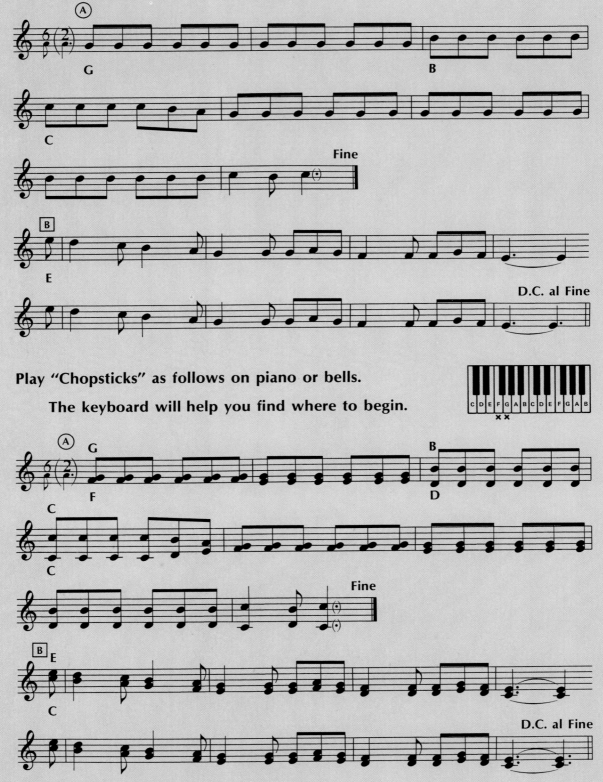

Play "Chopsticks" as follows on piano or bells.

The keyboard will help you find where to begin.

What is your birth date? Which month?
Which day? Which year? Write it down by using
numbers. Look at the line of numbers you have
written. Do you see any number twice in a row
(repeat)? Do you see two numbers side by side
that show a large interval? A small interval?

Play your number pattern on a melody instrument.
Decide which tone will be number 1 and play
upward and downward by step or by leap,
or repeat a tone as the numbers tell you.

Do you have a zero in your number line?
Play it as a percussion sound, or make it silent.

You can vary the pattern. Change the tempo.
Change the dynamics. Change the rhythm.
Change the starting note. Play the pattern backward.

Think of a way to write down your melody.

Play a drone accompaniment for "Namane Kare."

Pluck the C and G strings of an Autoharp

at the same time, over and over.

NAMANE KARE FOLK SONG FROM INDIA

USED BY PERMISSION OF WILLIAM M. ANDERSON.

Na - ma - ne ka - re cha - tu - re shi - ri gu - ru cha - ra - na,
(Nah-mah-nuh kah-ruh chah-too-ruh shee-ree goo-roo chah-rah-nah,

Ta - ne ma - ne ni - re - ma - le ka - re bha - ve ta - ra - na.
Tah-nuh mah-nuh nee-ruh-mah-luh kah-ruh bhah-vuh tah-rah-nah.

Na - ma - ne ka - re cha - tu - re shi - ri gu - ru cha - ra - na.
Nah-mah-nuh kah-ruh chah-too-ruh shee-ree goo-roo chah-rah-nah.)

WHAT DO YOU HEAR? 16: MELODY

Here are the melodies of some songs that you know.

Part of each melody is missing on the recording.

Listen and decide whether the missing part moves mostly

by step, by leap, or whether the tones repeat.

Listen. Then choose your answer.

1.	*America*	STEP	LEAP	REPEAT
2.	*Rookoombine*	STEP	LEAP	REPEAT
3.	*Rookoombine*	STEP	LEAP	REPEAT
4.	*The Star-Spangled Banner*	STEP	LEAP	REPEAT
5.	*Frère Jacques*	STEP	LEAP	REPEAT
6.	*Reveille*	STEP	LEAP	REPEAT

THE ARTS: CONTEMPORARY FORMING PROCESS

A computer helped the artist create this picture.

Look at the top line of drawings from left to right. It shows
several things in a row.

Look at the bottom line of drawings from left to right.
It shows how an artist can give a feeling of movement
from one thing to another.

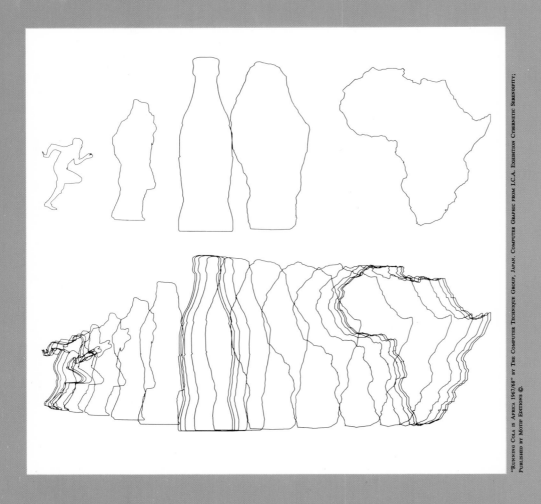

"Running Cola is Africa 1967/68" by The Computer Technique Group, Japan. Computer Graphic from I.C.A. Exhibition Cybernetic Serendipity; Published by Motif Editions ©.

A computer helped create this work also. The artist wanted to suggest movement from one thing to another. Look at the work from left to right. Try to feel it moving along.

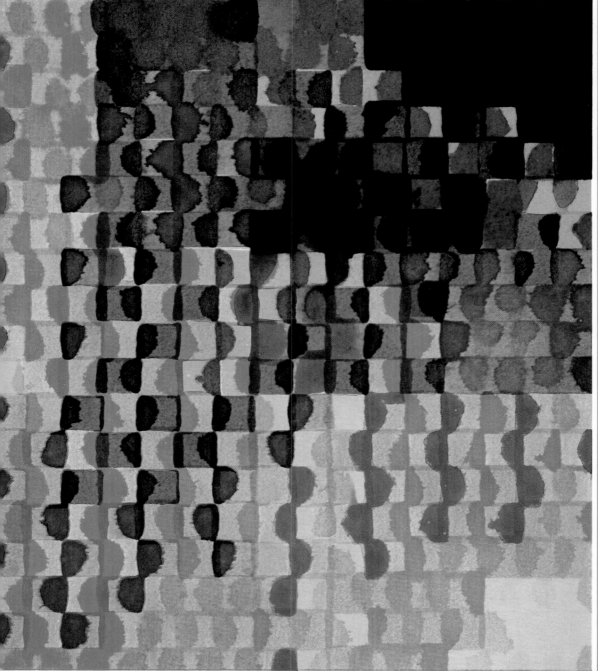

"Matrix Multiplication" by Frieder Nake. Courtesy, Bruckman-Verlag, Munich.

Music moves from moment to moment with sounds and silences.
You can feel and hear these as they move along from a beginning
to an end. Listen for the sounds and silences in this music.

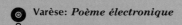 Varèse: *Poème électronique*
9

This chart will help you describe what you heard.

HIGH AND LOW SOUNDS	LOUD AND SOFT SOUNDS
UPWARD AND DOWNWARD DIRECTION	DIFFERENT TONE COLORS
PAUSES	THIN AND THICK DENSITY
FAST AND SLOW MOVEMENT	WIDE AND NARROW RANGE

Sounds and silences can be "formed" to do something as
they move along from a beginning to an end.

Follow the score on pages 204 and 205 as you listen to
Sound Piece 9. This piece was composed using a piano
melody and a tape recorder.

After you have listened, try creating your own sound piece
on a stereo tape recorder. Use voices or instruments or
both. The chart below will help you organize your ideas.

	10″	10″	10″	10″
Channel I	sound	silence	sound	silence

Now go back to the beginning of your 40-second piece. This time, fill
in the silences by recording new material on Channel II. Follow
the chart below, or think of something else to do.

Channel I	sound	silence	sound	silence
Channel II		Play at a different speed.		Slow down the feed reel.

SOUND PIECE 9: Theme and Tape Recorder
"Alteration"

JOYCE BOGUSKY-REIMER   © 1980 JOYCE BOGUSKY-REIMER

Theme

"Alteration"

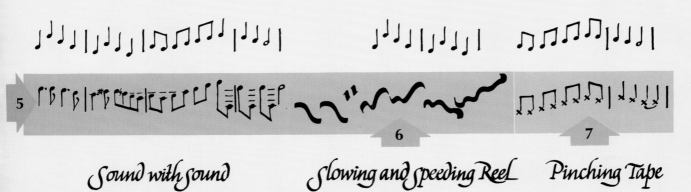

Sound with Sound   *Slowing and Speeding Reel*   *Pinching Tape*

METER

In some American Indian music you can hear and feel that the sets
of beats keep changing from 3 to 2. To help you hear this,
listen to the tom-tom accompaniment on the recording.

MUJE MUKESIN   OJIBWAY INDIAN TUNE

Mu - je muk - e - sin, aw - yaw - yon, Mu - je muk - e - sin, aw - yaw - yon,

Mu - je muk - e - sin, aw - yaw - yon, Mu - je muk - e - sin, aw - yaw - yon.

Play this pattern to accompany the song. Be certain to stress
the first beat—the strong beat—of each measure.

Sometimes sets of three beats and two beats are grouped together
in the same measure. When this happens, the music has a
meter in 5. Listen to this music. Try to feel the beats
grouped in sets of five. Listen for the strong beat at
the beginning of each set.

Desmond: *Take Five*

Play these patterns to accompany "Hineh mah tov."

Tambourine (music notation) (shake)

Drum (music notation)

Wood Block (music notation)

HINEH MAH TOV
HEBREW FOLK SONG

Hi-neh mah tov u-ma na - im, She-vet a-chim gam ya - chad.

Hi - neh mah_____ tov, She - vet a - chim gam ya - chad.

Can you find these patterns in "Hineh mah tov"?

1. (music notation)

2. (music notation)

3. (music notation)

4. (music notation)

Find the part of "Paddy Works on the Railway" that uses this rhythm pattern.

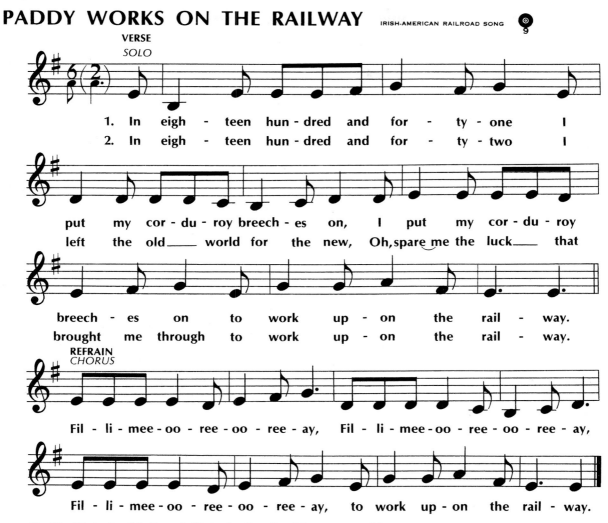

PADDY WORKS ON THE RAILWAY
IRISH-AMERICAN RAILROAD SONG

VERSE
SOLO

1. In eigh - teen hun - dred and for - ty - one I
2. In eigh - teen hun - dred and for - ty - two I

put my cor - du - roy breech - es on, I put my cor - du - roy
left the old___ world for the new, Oh, spare me the luck___ that

breech - es on to work up - on the rail - way.
brought me through to work up - on the rail - way.

REFRAIN
CHORUS

Fil - li - mee - oo - ree - oo - ree - ay, Fil - li - mee - oo - ree - oo - ree - ay,

Fil - li - mee - oo - ree - oo - ree - ay, to work up - on the rail - way.

3. It's "Pat, do this," and "Pat, do that," without a stocking or cravat,

And nothing but an old straw hat, while working on the railway. *Refrain*

Sing this countermelody during the refrain.

Countermelody

Fil' - mee - oo - ree - oo - ree - ay,___

Pad - dy works up - on the rail - way.

Meter 209

Notice how the beats in this song are divided.

ME AND MY BROTHER, OLIVER LEE

WORDS AND MUSIC BY FRED STARK

© 1972 FRED STARK. © 1979 ELEVEN EGGS MUSIC, INC. REPRINTED BY PERMISSION.

1. Most of the time we are hap - py and gay,
2. Leav - ing for school, be gone most of the day,
3. Home-ward we go a - gain, run - ning a - long, The

Laugh - in' and play - in' the hours_____ a - way,
Me and my broth - er, good - by we would say,
mis - chief we're in - to, hope it won't be wrong,

Spend - ing some time in the eve - ning at home with him._____
Laugh - in' and car - ry - in' on all the time with him._____
Soon we are say - in' our prayers at the end of day._____

Up in the morn - ing at break - ing of dawn,
Mak - in' our way through the day, he and I,
Off in - to slum - ber we slip right a - way,

We're hap - py to - geth - er 'most all the day long,_____
I need help with home-work, he'll give it a try,_____
'Cause to - mor - row's an - oth - er won - der - ful day,_____

210 Meter

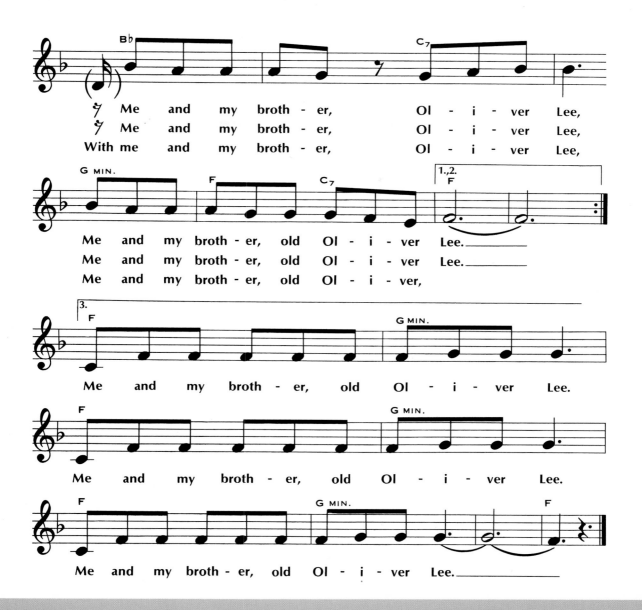

Me and my broth - er, Ol - i - ver Lee,
Me and my broth - er, Ol - i - ver Lee,
With me and my broth - er, Ol - i - ver Lee,

Me and my broth - er, old Ol - i - ver Lee.
Me and my broth - er, old Ol - i - ver Lee.
Me and my broth - er, old Ol - i - ver,

Me and my broth - er, old Ol - i - ver Lee.

Me and my broth - er, old Ol - i - ver Lee.

Me and my broth - er, old Ol - i - ver Lee.

Play these parts to accompany "Me and My Brother, Oliver Lee."

As you play, feel the steady beat divided into threes.

Drum

Tambourine

Listen for the steady beat divided into threes in this music.

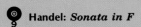 Handel: *Sonata in F*

1. Si - lent night, ho - ly night, All is calm,
2. Si - lent night, ho - ly night, Shep - herds quake

all is bright Round yon Vir - gin Moth - er and Child.
at the sight, Glo - ries stream — from heav - en a - far,

Ho - ly In - fant so ten - der and mild, Sleep in heav - en - ly
Heav'n - ly hosts — sing "Al - le - lu - ia, Christ the Sav - ior is

peace, _____ Sleep __ in heav - en - ly peace. _____
born! _____ Christ __ the Sav - ior is born!" _____

Play the Autoharp to accompany "Silent Night." Use this strumming pattern, or create one of your own.

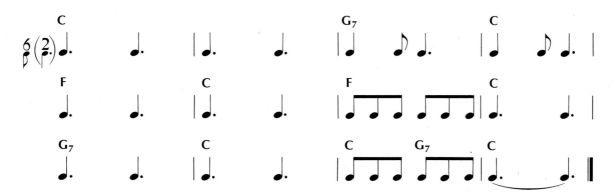

Can you hear meter in this music? Each time a number is called, decide whether the meter is in 2, 3, or 5. Listen. Then choose your answer.

	METER IN	METER IN	METER IN	
1.	2	3	5	Telemann: *Suite in A Minor for Flute and String Orchestra*
2.	2	3	5	Britten: *Matinées Musicales*
3.	2	3	5	Desmond: *Take Five*
4.	2	3	5	Gould: *American Salute*
5.	2	3	5	*The Star-Spangled Banner*
6.	2	3	5	Tchaikovsky: *Capriccio Italien*
7.	2	3	5	Haydn: *String Quartet*, Op. 76

PHRASES

214

4

As you listen to the recording
of this Hawaiian chant,
move your arms to show
the length of each phrase.

HE MELE O KE KAHULI FOLK SONG FROM HAWAII

Ka - hu - li a - ku, Ka - hu - li mai,

Ka - hu - li lei u - la, Lei a - ko - le - a,

Ko - le - a, ko - le - a, Ho - i - ka wai

Wai a - ko - le - a, Ko - le - a, ko - le - a.

When you move to the Hawaiian chant "He mele o ke kahuli,"

you can feel that each phrase is the same length.

Can you discover what is the same about each phrase in this song?

HARVESTING TEA
FOLK SONG FROM JAPAN   ENGLISH WORDS BY RAYMOND MATTHEWS

1. When sum-mer comes up-on the moun-tains and the val - leys,
2. And as they pick each rip-ened leaf so ver-y gent - ly,

And cov-ers ev - 'ry-thing with fresh and ten-der young, green leaves,
They sing a song of joy; the air is filled with mel - o - dy;

Then it is time for all the peo-ple of the vil - lage
Their hap-py song is car-ried on the sum-mer breez - es;

To gath - er in the fields to har - vest leaves for tea.
It says it's time a - gain to har - vest leaves for tea.

Play this countermelody as others sing "Harvesting Tea."

Recorder or Bells

Sing the chorus parts when they come in this song. Will you sing long phrases, or short phrases?

JANE, JANE AMERICAN FOLK SONG

REPRINTED FROM SING OUT! THE FOLK SONG MAGAZINE, 505 EIGHTH AVE., NEW YORK, N.Y. 10018. USED WITH PERMISSION.

SOLO 1. Hey, hey,___ CHORUS Jane, Jane, SOLO My Lord - y, Lord, CHORUS Jane, Jane,

SOLO I'm___ a-gon-na buy, CHORUS Jane, Jane, SOLO Three mock - ing birds, CHORUS Jane, Jane,

SOLO One___ a - for to whis-tle, CHORUS Jane, Jane, SOLO One___ a-for to sing, CHORUS Jane, Jane,

SOLO One___ a-for to do, CHORUS Jane, Jane, SOLO Most an - y lit - tle thing, CHORUS Jane, Jane.

2. Hey, hey, Jane, Jane,
   My Lordy, Lord, Jane, Jane,
   I'm a-gonna buy, Jane, Jane,
   Three hunting dogs, Jane, Jane,
   One a-for to run, Jane, Jane,
   One a-for to shout, Jane, Jane,
   One to talk to, Jane, Jane,
   When I go out, Jane, Jane.

3. Hey, hey, . . .
   My Lordy, Lord, . . .
   I'm a-gonna buy, . . .
   Three muley cows, . . .
   One a-for to milk, . . .
   One to plough my corn, . . .
   One a-for to pray, . . .
   On Christmas morn, . . .

4. Hey, hey, . . .
   My Lordy, Lord, . . .
   I'm a-gonna buy, . . .
   Three little blue birds, . . .
   One a-for to weep, . . .
   One a-for to mourn, . . .
   One a-for to grieve, . . .
   When I am gone, . . .

Which phrases are long?

Which phrases are short?

THREE WHITE GULLS

FOLK SONG FROM ITALY   ENGLISH WORDS BY MARGUERITE WILKINSON

ORIGINAL TITLE "THE THREE DOVES" BY MARGUERITE WILKINSON FROM BOTSFORD COLLECTION OF FOLK SONGS—VOLUME 3. COPYRIGHT © 1921, 1922 G. SCHIRMER, INC. USED BY PERMISSION.

1. There are three_____ white gulls_____ a - fly - ing;
2. In the waves_____ they dip_____ their soft wings;

There are three_____ white gulls_____ a - fly - ing;
In the waves_____ they dip_____ their soft_____ wings;

There are three_____ white gulls a - fly - ing;_____
In the waves_____ they dip their soft wings;_____

By the sea they cry, By the sea they cry, By the sea they cry.
Then__ soar to the sky, Then__ soar to the sky, Then__ soar to the sky.

There are three_____ white gulls a - fly - ing;_____
In the waves_____ they dip their soft wings;_____

By the sea they cry, By the sea they cry, By the sea they cry.
Then__ soar to the sky, Then__ soar to the sky, Then__ soar to the sky.

Find the phrases in this song that are sequences.

NINE RED HORSEMEN

FOLK MELODY FROM MEXICO   WORDS BY ELEANOR FARJEON

FROM ELEANOR FARJEON'S POEMS FOR CHILDREN. ORIGINALLY PUBLISHED IN SING FOR YOUR SUPPER BY ELEANOR FARJEON, COPYRIGHT, 1938, BY ELEANOR FARJEON, RENEWED 1966 BY GERVASE FARJEON. BY PERMISSION OF J.B. LIPPINCOTT, PUBLISHERS; AND HAROLD OBER ASSOCIATES, INCORPORATED.

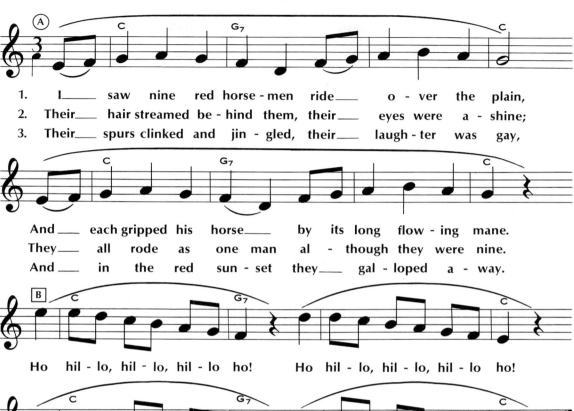

1. I____ saw nine red horse-men ride____ o-ver the plain,
2. Their____ hair streamed be-hind them, their____ eyes were a-shine;
3. Their____ spurs clinked and jin-gled, their____ laugh-ter was gay,

And ____ each gripped his horse____ by its long flow-ing mane.
They____ all rode as one man al-though they were nine.
And ____ in the red sun-set they____ gal-loped a-way.

Ho hil-lo, hil-lo, hil-lo ho!   Ho hil-lo, hil-lo, hil-lo ho!

Ho hil-lo, hil-lo, hil-lo ho!   Ho hil-lo, hil-lo, hil-lo ho!

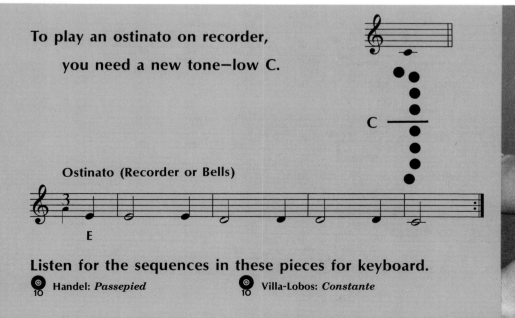

To play an ostinato on recorder, you need a new tone—low C.

C

Ostinato (Recorder or Bells)

E

Listen for the sequences in these pieces for keyboard.

Handel: *Passepied*   Villa-Lobos: *Constante*

Listen for the phrases in section A of this song. Do you hear strong cadences, weak cadences, or a combination of strong and weak?

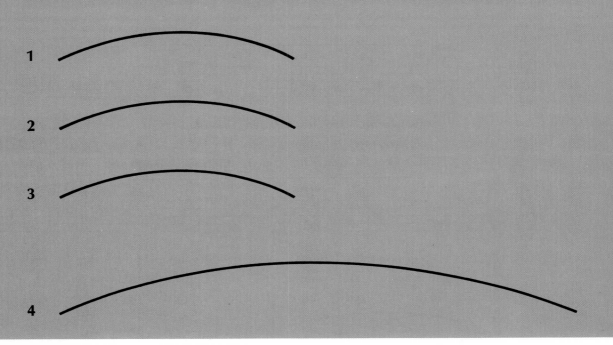

OH, WHAT A BEAUTIFUL CITY

BLACK SPIRITUAL

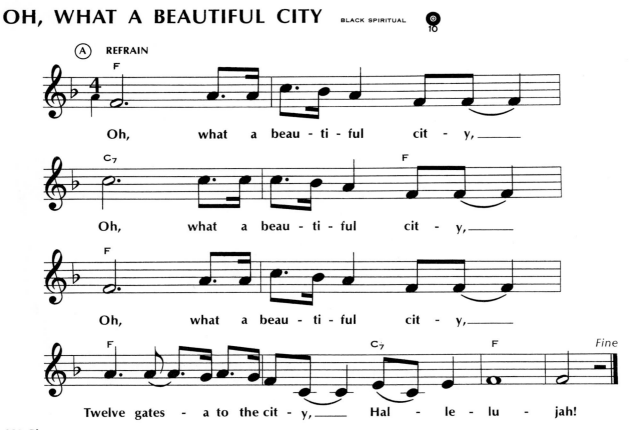

Oh, what a beau - ti - ful cit - y, _____

Oh, what a beau - ti - ful cit - y, _____

Oh, what a beau - ti - ful cit - y, _____

Twelve gates - a to the cit - y, _____ Hal - le - lu - jah!

Listen for the combination of weak and strong cadences in section B.

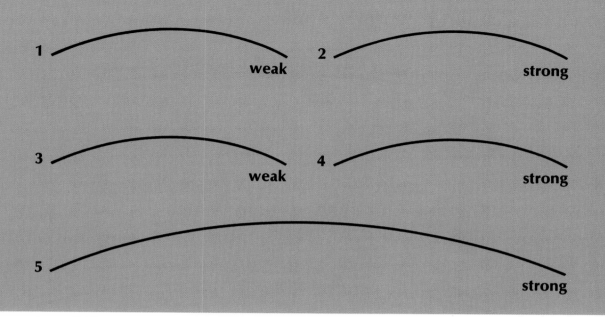

1   weak   2   strong

3   weak   4   strong

5   strong

B   VERSE

Three gates ___ to the East,

Three gates ___ to the West,

Three gates ___ to the North, _____

Three gates ___ to the South,

D.C. al Fine

There's twelve gates - a to the cit - y, ___ Hal - le - lu - jah!

Choose one of the phrases below. Play each event on the instrument named. "Play" the phrase again, silently.

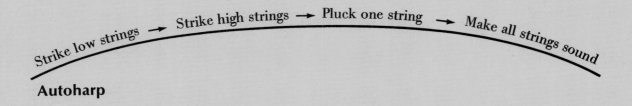

Strike low strings → Strike high strings → Pluck one string → Make all strings sound

Autoharp

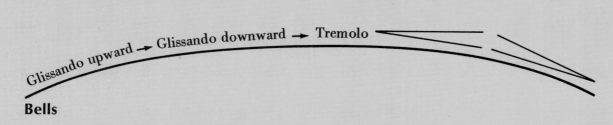

Glissando upward → Glissando downward → Tremolo

Bells

Glissando upward—Pull mallet across bells from lowest to highest.

Glissando downward—Pull mallet across bells from highest to lowest.

Tremolo—Play any two bells together, striking them

rapidly over and over.

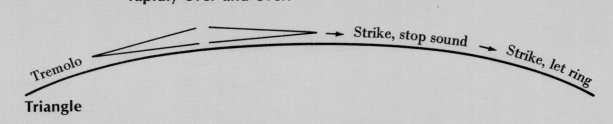

Tremolo → Strike, stop sound → Strike, let ring

Triangle

Tremolo—With beater inside triangle, use a circular

motion to strike the three sides over and over.

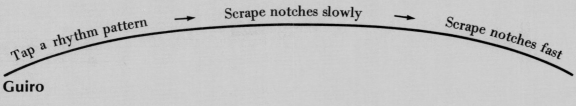

Tap a rhythm pattern → Scrape notches slowly → Scrape notches fast

Guiro

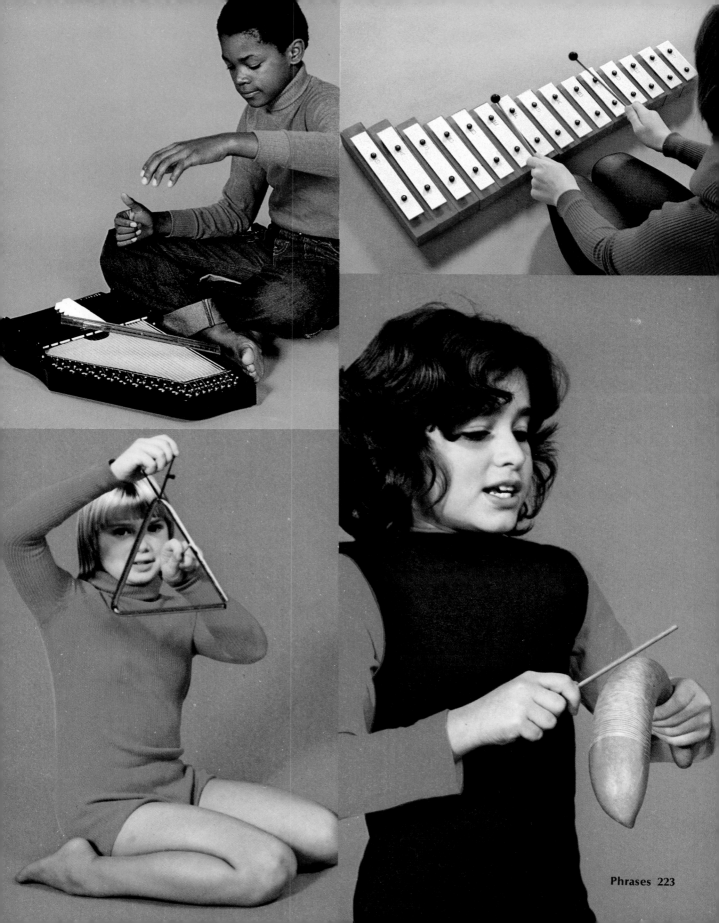

STYLE: POLYNESIAN

Because people moved from island to island, the music of Polynesia spread from tribe to tribe. Look at the map to see the names of some of the islands. The people there sing and dance the stories and legends they love so well.

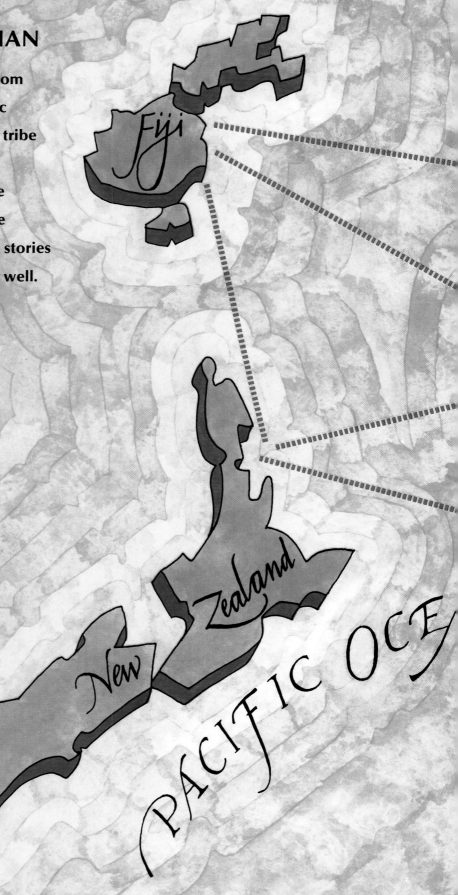

Fiji

New Zealand

PACIFIC OCE

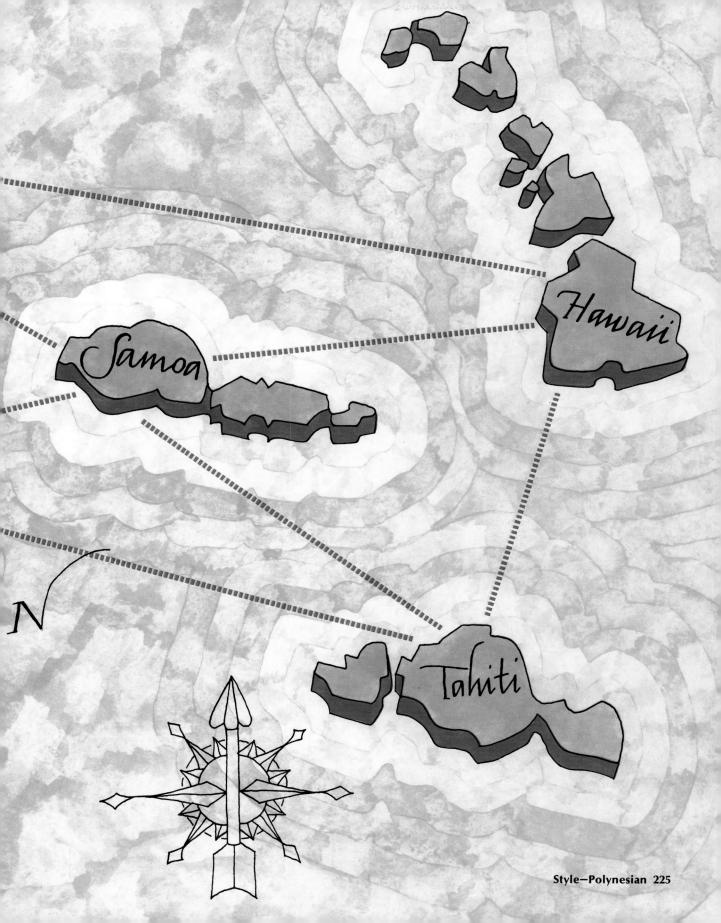

Samoa

Hawaii

Tahiti

N

Listen to these chants. The first is from
Hawaii. The second is from Tahiti.

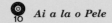 *Ai a la o Pele*

🔟 *Tahitian Chant*

You will find another Polynesian song on
page 215 in your book. Play this
rhythm pattern on a gourd or ipu as
an accompaniment.

$\frac{4}{}$

hit with   hit with   heel   tip   tip
heel of   finger
hand   tips

Polynesian music uses chant, rhythm, and
movement to create a style of its own.

TONALITY—ATONALITY

Listen to the bugle call *Reveille*. Try to hear how the music

focuses on one important tone.

 Reveille

Now play *Reveille* on the bells D, G, B. As you play, feel the pull

toward the tonal center, G.

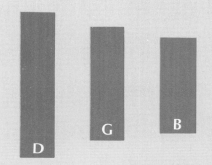

REVEILLE

When you played *Reveille,* you used three different tones.

Now play a melody that uses twelve different tones.

Take the bells from C to B out of the box

and arrange them as follows:

A$^\sharp$ A B C$^\sharp$ D C D$^\sharp$ F E F$^\sharp$ G$^\sharp$ G

Play the bells from left to right. Use any rhythm you choose.

Is there a pull toward a tonal center in this melody?

Is there a focus on one important tone?

Bugle calls and fanfares are often used to announce important events.
The first fanfare you will hear was used for many important
ceremonies in England several hundred years ago.
The second one was used to open the New York State Theater at
The Lincoln Center for the Performing Arts in New York City.
Which is tonal? Which is atonal?

Purcell: *Fanfare*   Stravinsky: *Fanfare for Two Trumpets*

Here are the endings of two songs you know. They each have a
pull toward a tonal center. Do they end on the same tone,
or on different tones?

1.

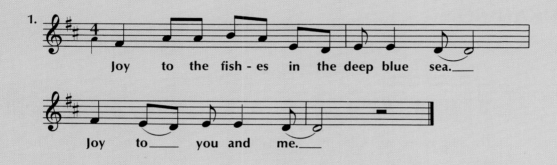

Joy   to the fish - es   in the deep blue   sea.___

Joy   to___   you and   me.___

2.

Bet - ter keep your hand   right   on___   that plow,___

Hold   on,   hold   on,   hold   on.

Both songs are tonal. Both songs end on D. Yet each song
 has a different general sound or tonality.
"Joy to the World" has a major tonality.
"Hold On" has a minor tonality.
Each song uses a different arrangement of tones, or scale.

Play these major and minor scales on bells.

MAJOR	D E F# G A B C# D
MINOR	D E F G A B♭ C D

As you sing "Chanukah Song," decide whether the tonality is
major or minor.

CHANUKAH SONG
HASIDIC FOLK SONG   ENGLISH WORDS BY ALICE FIRGAU

'Tis the week of Cha - nu - kah, Good cheer it is bring - ing. This
hol - i - day we cel - e - brate in danc - ing and sing - ing.

Gath - er round to - geth - er, the ho - ra we'll do;

Then join in a song that our fore - fath - ers knew. But

hush now and come now, The can - dles we light one by

one. Then hear the sto - ry of God and His glo - ry And

how pre - cious free - dom was won.

Listen to the recording. Each time a number is called, choose the word that describes the tonality. Is the music tonal, or atonal? Listen. Then choose your answer.

---

1. *TONAL*   *ATONAL*   Prokofiev: *Classical Symphony,* "Gavotte"

---

2. *TONAL*   *ATONAL*   Webern: *Five Movements for String Quartet*

---

3. *TONAL*   *ATONAL*   Stravinsky: *Fanfare for Two Trumpets*

---

4. *TONAL*   *ATONAL*   Beethoven: *Symphony No. 9*

---

5. *TONAL*   *ATONAL*   Purcell: *Fanfare*

---

6. *TONAL*   *ATONAL*   Mozart: *Symphony No. 40*

There can be many arrangements of tones within an octave.

Play the major scale starting on G. Then play the pentatonic scale.

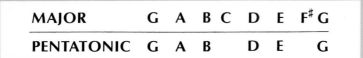

MAJOR	G A B C D E F♯ G
PENTATONIC	G A B D E G

Here are two songs that you know. Sing them to hear which matches the general sound of the major scale and which matches the general sound of the pentatonic scale.

"The Frog in the Well," p. 178

"Harvesting Tea," p. 216

Play this pentatonic melody on recorder or bells.

You will need these five tones.

Practice them before you play.

Recorder

D E G A B

AN IROQUOIS LULLABY

IROQUOIS INDIAN SONG 10

FROM CANADA'S STORY IN SONG BY EDITH FOWKE AND ALAN MILLS, © GAGE PUBLISHING 1965. REPRINTED BY PERMISSION.

Ho, ho,___ wa - ta - nay, Ho, ho,___ wa - ta - nay,

Ho, ho,___ wa - ta - nay, Ki - yo - ke - na, ki - yo - ke - na.

This song from China is sung at New Year's celebrations.

The melody is based on the pentatonic scale. Sing it or play it on recorder or bells. You will need these five tones.

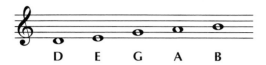

D E G A B

COLORFUL BOATS

FOLK SONG FROM CHINA   ENGLISH VERSION BY CAROL KERR

COPYRIGHT © 1979, WILLIAM M. ANDERSON. USED BY PERMISSION.

Tsai lung chuan yia me yia wei yao,
See the bright col-ored har - bor boats,

Lai da mang yao___ yia he hei,
Dec - o - rat - ed for fes - ti - val,

Lai dau tze li bien yia wei tze yao,
Come to watch as they dance on the waves;

Lai bai nien yao hua tze,
Cel - e - brate the New Year,

Yai he hai hai yao he hei,
Sing to-geth - er, sing with joy,

Lai bai nien yao hua tze.
Cel - e - brate the New Year.

Look at these scale diagrams. Notice how they are alike and how
they are different. Then play the scales on bells.

MAJOR	C D E F G A B C
WHOLE TONE	C D E F# G# A# C

Play "Frère Jacques" as a major melody, using the tones of the
major scale.

FRERE JACQUES (Major)

Now play "Frère Jacques" as a whole-tone melody, using the tones
of the whole-tone scale.

FRERE JACQUES (Whole Tone)

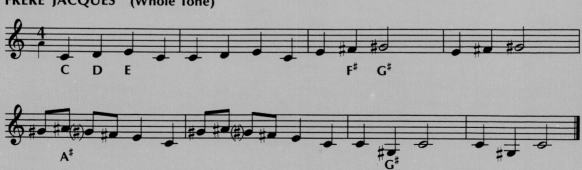

Each scale has a different general sound. A melody has the same
general sound as the scale it is based on.

Listen to this song. Is the melody based on a major scale, or a whole-tone scale?

END OF SUMMER

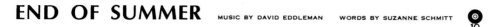

MUSIC BY DAVID EDDLEMAN   WORDS BY SUZANNE SCHMITT

Swim - ming, _ Build - ing cas - tles Out ___ of sand ___ at the shore.

Till the tide comes wash - ing a - way Sum - mer, ___

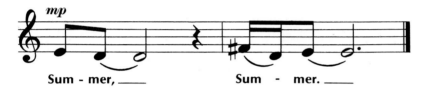

Sum - mer, ___   Sum - mer. ___

The lyrics of "End of Summer" form a five-line poem called a *cinquain.* The lines of a cinquain follow this pattern of syllables: 2-4-6-8-2.

END OF SUMMER

Swimming, (2)

Building castles (4)

Out of sand at the shore. (6)

Till the tide comes washing away (8)

Summer. (2)

Suzanne Schmitt

Make up your own whole-tone melody for the poem.

THE ARTS: FOCUS, NO FOCUS

In some paintings your eyes travel to one important place—a center
of interest, or focus.

Which of these paintings has such a focus? Which has not?

GEORGIA O'KEEFFE. THE WHITE FLOWER. (1931.) OIL ON CANVAS. 30 x 36 INCHES. COLLECTION OF THE WHITNEY MUSEUM OF AMERICAN ART. PURCHASE.

BROOKS: TONDO.

In some music your ears hear one tone as most important (tonal music).

The music comes to rest on that tone.

Some music does not have a tonal center (atonal music).

Listen to these pieces. Which is tonal? Which is atonal?

 Webern: *Five Movements for String Quartet*   Mozart: *Divertimento in D*

CALL CHART 9: TEXTURE

Listen for the different textures in some music you know.

The chart will help you hear them.

---

1. MELODY ALONE

Amazing Grace

---

2. MELODY WITH COUNTERMELODY

Michael Finnegan

---

3. MELODY WITH CHORDS

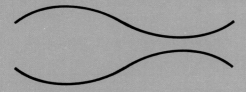

Me and My Brother, Oliver Lee

---

4. MELODY SUNG AS A ROUND

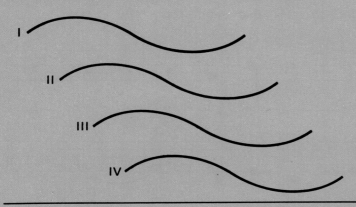

Up the Street the Band Is Marching Down

Use different textures when you perform "This Land Is Your Land."

1. Sing the melody alone.

THIS LAND IS YOUR LAND

WORDS AND MUSIC BY WOODY GUTHRIE   COUNTERMELODY BY RUTH TUTELMAN

REFRAIN   Bb   F

This land is your land,_____ this land is my land,_____

C7   F

From Ca - li - for - nia_____ to the New York is - land;_____

Bb   F

From the red - wood for - est_____ to the Gulf Stream wa - ters;_____

C7   F   Fine

This land was made for you and me._____

VERSE   Bb   F

1. As I was walk - ing_____ that rib - bon of high - way,_____

C7   F

I saw a - bove me_____ that end - less sky - way._____

Bb   F

I saw be - low me_____ that gold - en val - ley,_____

C7   F   D.C. al Fine

This land was made for you and me._____

2. I've roamed and rambled and I followed my footsteps

To the sparkling sands of her diamond deserts,

And all around me a voice was sounding,

"This land was made for you and me." *Refrain*

3. When the sun comes shining and I was strolling

And the wheatfields waving and the dust clouds rolling,

As the fog was lifting a voice was chanting,

"This land was made for you and me." *Refrain*

2. Sing the melody with Autoharp accompaniment.

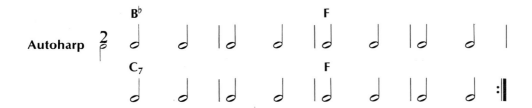

3. Add this countermelody when you sing the refrain.

COUNTERMELODY (Refrain)

This land is your land, this land is mine,

From Maine to Mon - ta - na, des - ert to the shore,

We sing that this land is your land, this land is mine,

Yes, it's made for you and me. _____

When you know this song, sing it as a round. This will make the density of the music thicker. For an even thicker density, add the parts for bells or recorder to your singing.

THE GHOST OF JOHN

WORDS AND MUSIC BY MARTHA GRUBB

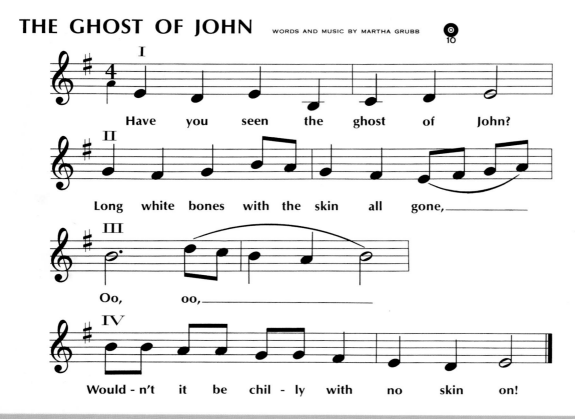

I
Have you seen the ghost of John?

II
Long white bones with the skin all gone, _____

III
Oo, oo, _____

IV
Would - n't it be chil - ly with no skin on!

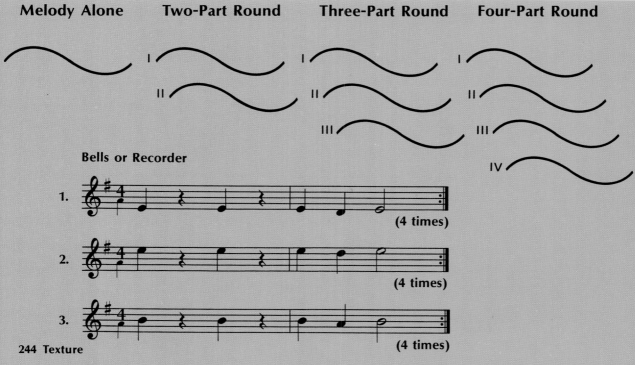

Melody Alone   Two-Part Round   Three-Part Round   Four-Part Round

Bells or Recorder

1. (4 times)

2. (4 times)

3. (4 times)

Perform this song using various textures. Is the density thin, or thick?

PSALM OF THANKSGIVING

DAKOTA INDIAN HYMN   MUSICAL SETTING BY CARLTON YOUNG

ENGLISH WORDS BY PHILIP FRAZIER

1. Man - y and great, O God, are Thy things, Mak - er of
2. Grant un - to us com - mu - nion with Thee, Thou star - a -

earth and sky;____ Thy hands have set the heav - ens with stars;
bid - ing One;____ Come un - to us and dwell with____ us

Thy fin - gers spread the moun - tains and plains.____ Lo, at Thy
With Thee are found the gifts of____ life.____ Bless us with

word the wa - ters were formed; Deep seas o - bey Thy voice.
life that has no____ end, E - ter - nal life with Thee.

Recorder

(6 times)

Autoharp Drone (to be plucked an octave lower)

Perform this song two ways: 1. as a melody alone

2. as a melody with chords

HE'S GOT THE WHOLE WORLD IN HIS HANDS

BLACK SPIRITUAL

1. He's got the whole world_____ in his hands,_____
2. He's got the wind and rain_____ in his hands,_____
3. He's got both you and me_____ in his hands,_____

He's got the whole world_____ in his hands,_____
He's got the wind and rain_____ in his hands,_____
He's got both you and me_____ in his hands,_____

He's got the whole world_____ in his hands,_____
He's got the wind and rain_____ in his hands,_____
He's got both you and me_____ in his hands,_____

He's got the whole world in his hands._____
He's got the whole world in his hands._____
He's got the whole world in his hands._____

Autoharp

WHAT DO YOU HEAR? 19: TEXTURE ⊚

Listen to this music. Sometimes you will hear a melody with guitar accompaniment. The density of the sound will be thin. Sometimes you will hear a vocal or instrumental countermelody along with the melody and accompaniment. The density of the sound will be thicker. Each time a number is called, choose the answer that describes the texture you hear.

Makem: *Winds of Morning*

---

1. MELODY WITH ACCOMPANIMENT   COUNTERMELODY ADDED
THIN DENSITY   THICKER DENSITY

---

2. MELODY WITH ACCOMPANIMENT   COUNTERMELODY ADDED
THIN DENSITY   THICKER DENSITY

---

3. MELODY WITH ACCOMPANIMENT   COUNTERMELODY ADDED
THIN DENSITY   THICKER DENSITY

---

4. MELODY WITH ACCOMPANIMENT   COUNTERMELODY ADDED
THIN DENSITY   THICKER DENSITY

---

5. MELODY WITH ACCOMPANIMENT   COUNTERMELODY ADDED
THIN DENSITY   THICKER DENSITY

---

6. MELODY WITH ACCOMPANIMENT   COUNTERMELODY ADDED
THIN DENSITY   THICKER DENSITY

THE ARTS: DENSITY

These two paintings are by the same artist. What do you notice
about the top part of each? What do you notice about
the bottom part of each?

The density of what you see is an important part of how a
painting feels.

TANGUY, YVES. MAMA, PAPA IS WOUNDED!, 1927. OIL ON CANVAS, 36¼ x 28¾". COLLECTION, THE MUSEUM OF MODERN ART, NEW YORK.

Tanguy, Yves. Multiplication des Arcs, 1954. Oil on canvas, 40 x 60". Collection, The Museum of Modern Art, New York. Mrs. Simon Guggenheim Fund.

Music has density, too. Listen to two pieces by the same
composer. What do you notice about the density of each one?

Copland: *Statements*   Copland: *Music for a Great City*

Density in painting can be made by having open spaces (thin)
or by crowding many things into a space (thick).

Density in music can be made by having only a few sounds
(thin) or by piling up sounds together (thick).

Each art creates a feeling of thin or thick in its own way.

RECORDER FINGERING CHART

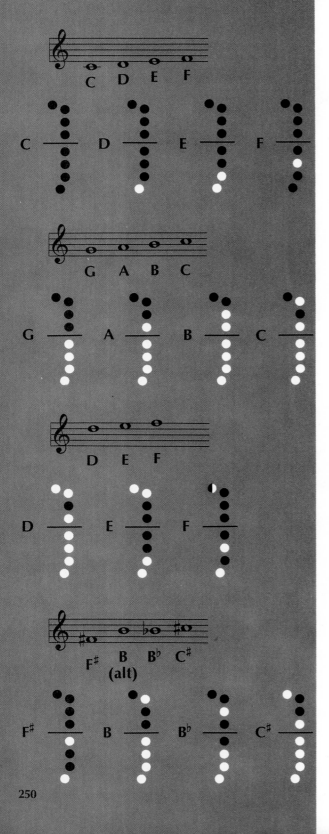

GLOSSARY

accent A single tone or chord louder than those around it

accompaniment Music that supports the sound of a solo performer

atonal Music in which no single tone is a "home base" or "resting place"

ballad In music, a song that tells a story

beat A repeating pulse that can be felt in some music

cadence A group of chords or notes at the end of a phrase or piece that gives a feeling of pausing or finishing

chord Three or more different tones played or sung together

chord pattern An arrangement of chords into a small grouping, usually occurring often in a piece

cluster A group of tones very close together performed at the same time; used mostly in modern music

composer A person who makes up pieces of music by putting sounds together in his or her own way

contour The "shape" of a melody, made by the way it moves upward and downward in steps and leaps, and by repeated tones

contrast Two or more things that are different. In music, slow is a *contrast* to fast; section A is a *contrast* to section B.

countermelody A melody that is played or sung at the same time as the main melody

density The thickness or thinness of sound

drone An accompaniment made up of a tone or tones that are repeated or sustained throughout a piece of music

dynamics The loudness and softness of sound

elements The parts out of which whole works of art are made: for example, music uses the *elements* melody, rhythm, texture, tone color, form; painting uses line, color, space, shape, etc.

ensemble A group of players or singers

form The overall plan of a piece of music

ground A melody pattern repeated over and over in the bass (lowest part) of a piece, while other things happen above it

harmony Two or more tones sounding at the same time

improvisation Making up music as it is being performed; often used in jazz

measure A grouping of beats set off by bar lines

melody A line of single tones that move upward, downward, or repeat

melody pattern An arrangement of pitches into a small grouping, usually occurring often in a piece

meter The way the beats of music are grouped, often in sets of two or in sets of three

notes Symbols for sound in music

octave The distance of eight steps from one tone to another that has the same letter name. On the staff these steps are shown by the lines and spaces. When notes are an *octave* apart, there are eight lines and spaces from one note to the other.

pattern In the arts, an arrangement of an element or elements into a grouping, usually occurring often in the work (*see* elements)

phrase A musical "sentence." Each *phrase* expresses one thought. Music is made up of *phrases* that follow one another in a way that sounds right.

pitch The highness or lowness of a tone

range In a melody, the span from the lowest tone to the highest tone

register The pitch location of a group of tones (*see* pitch). If the group of tones are all high sounds, they are in a high *register*. If the group of tones are all low sounds, they are in a low *register*.

repetition Music that is the same, or almost the same, as music that was heard earlier

rests Symbols for silences in music

rhythm The way movement is organized in a piece of music, using beat, no beat, long and short sounds, meter, accents, no accents, tempo, syncopation, etc.

rhythm pattern A pattern of long and short sounds

scale An arrangement of pitches from lower to higher according to a specific pattern of intervals. Major, minor, pentatonic, and whole-tone are four kinds of scales. Each one has its own arrangement of pitches.

sequence The repetition of a melody pattern at a higher or lower pitch level

staff A set of five horizontal lines on which music notes are written

style The overall effect a work of art makes by the way its elements are used (*see* elements). When works of art use elements similarly, they are said to be "in the same style."

syncopation An arrangement of rhythm in which prominent or important tones begin on weak beats or weak parts of beats, giving a catchy, "off-balance" movement to the music

tempo The speed of the beat in a piece of music (*see* beat)

texture The way melody and harmony go together: a melody alone, two or more melodies together, or a melody with chords

theme An important melody that occurs several times in a piece of music

tonal Music that focuses on one tone that is more important than the others—a "home base" or "resting" tone

tone color The special sound that makes one instrument or voice sound different from another

triplet A rhythm pattern made by dividing a beat into three equal sounds

variation Music that is repeated but changed in some important way

vibration Back-and-forth motion that makes sound

INDEX

PICTURE CREDITS

3 4 5 6 7 8 9 10—RRD—88 87 86 85 84 83 82